Glasgow's
Grand Central Hotel

GLASGOW'S
MOST LOVED HOTEL

Glasgow's Grand Central Hotel

GLASGOW'S MOST LOVED HOTEL

WAVERLEY BOOKS

Published by Waverley Books, 144 Port Dundas Road, Glasgow G4 0HZ with the
Grand Central Hotel, 99 Gordon Street, Glasgow G1 3SL

This arrangement copyright © Waverley Books 2012

Text copyright © 2012 Jill Scott and Bill Hicks with additional material
copyright © 2012 Waverley Books Ltd

The photographs and illustrations contained within this book are the copyright of the
providers and may not be reproduced without permission from the copyright holders.

The publishers gratefully acknowledge the help and input of Laurie Nicol, General
Manager of the Grand Central Hotel, the management and staff past and present of
the Central Hotel, and the many individuals who have shared their memories with the
authors. We also wish to thank *The Herald* and *Evening Times*, Christine McGilly and
Patricia Grant and The Mitchell Library, and D C Thomson & Co Ltd. for research
and permission to use archival material.

Concept, design and layout, and additional photography: Mark Mechan
Editor: Penny Grearson
Picture research: Shona McGinlay

A catalogue record for this book is available from the British Library.

ISBN 978-1-84934-220-9

Printed and bound in the EU.

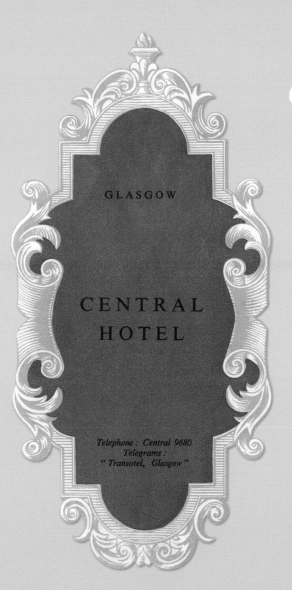

GLASGOW

CENTRAL
HOTEL

Telephone : Central 9680
Telegrams :
" Transotel, Glasgow "

Contents

Foreword

by Alex Salmond
Scotland's First Minister

The Central Hotel has been a Glasgow landmark since it opened in 1883. It has played host to show business stars such as Laurel and Hardy and Frank Sinatra, politicians such as John F Kennedy and Winston Churchill; and of course to thousands of people from Glasgow and beyond wanting to enjoy its public rooms. The hotel also has a permanent link to Scotland's great history of inventiveness and creativity, as the venue in 1927 for one of the transformational events of the 20th century, when John Logie Baird made the first-ever long-distance television broadcast from London to a room on the fourth floor.

Like many buildings with such a fascinating past, the hotel's history has also been embellished over the years by additional local legends – particularly the stories of the ghosts which are supposed to stay on its seventh floor.

I was delighted to have the honour of reopening the Grand Central Hotel on 20 January 2011. The refurbishment strikes a fitting balance between historic and modern – providing 21st century luxury and comfort, but retaining the essence of the hotel's historic glamour and grandeur. The restored hotel also adds to the range of top class hospitality venues which visitors and residents can enjoy in Glasgow.

I take great satisfaction when beautiful and iconic buildings like the Grand Central Hotel are restored. This book provides a fascinating insight into the rich history of this famous hotel and I hope it continues to serve guests long into the future.

Introduction

by Tony Troy
Chief Executive Officer, Principal Hayley

It gives me great pleasure every time I visit the Grand Central Hotel to see it properly restored to its rightful position as the Grand Dame of Glasgow hotels.

I first tried to buy the hotel fifteeen years ago on behalf of Principal Hotels but unfortunately did not succeed then. During the period of time between then and us acquiring the property, it had declined to such a sad state that there was a need for closure with total refurbishment. It is wonderful to see the hotel full of life today and operating at the top of the Glasgow hotel market.

We are very grateful for all the assistance we have received from the authorities in Glasgow and a particular word of thanks to Scotland's First Minister Alex Salmond who very kindly re-opened the hotel in January 2011. I wish the hotel every success and feel honoured to be involved in restoring the Grand Central to its rightful position with particular thanks to Laurie Nicol and her wonderful team.

A Few Thoughts from the Authors

A few years ago, while working as a newspaper reporter, I visited a company with a view to writing a feature on them. Founded by a family and built up by them, it had since passed from their hands. Some anecdotes from the company's history or old images would have made the story so much more interesting but I was told there were none. 'We are not interested in where we came from, we are only interested in where we are going,' were the very words used.

I came away saddened at how a company's history had been assigned to the rubbish bin by its new owners. Thankfully, Principal Hayley had the opposite view on the Grand Central Hotel's 130-year-old history or this book would never have been written and I feel very privileged to have been part of it.

It is a story which deserves to be told and the memories of times spent under its roof by many individuals recorded. Versions of times and events relying totally on memory might differ between people but are worth telling nevertheless. My own first memory of the hotel was when I was sent, along with a photographer, to see the late Sir Jimmy Savile when he was staying there in the 1970s. He greeted me with the words, 'I was told this was how I had to dress when I came to Glasgow, is it ok?'

He was wearing a top he'd had specially made with Celtic stripes on one side and Rangers colours on the other!

Both my parents, John and Grace Kinniburgh, have long since passed away but I feel in their own way they have somehow had an input into this book. My mother loved anything to do with Glasgow and my sister, Elizabeth, unearthed a suitcase from the attic full of books and notes she'd made on the history of the city which I have used as a source of information. My father always said you learned more from listening to people than talking to them and I have listened to many much treasured memories of times spent in the Central Hotel.

As well as its contents, the old battered suitcase is a relic from the history of a past railway company having had, at some time, an LMS sticker stamped on it. Where my parents journeyed to by train with this suitcase in the days before British Rail was formed in 1948 I can only imagine. Maybe before their train steamed down the track they had afternoon tea at the Central Hotel. I like to think they had enjoyed such a treat within its walls.

Scottish writer Thomas Carlyle (1795–1881) said, 'Nothing builds self-esteem and self-confidence like accomplishment.'

And the Grand Central Hotel has accomplished much to be proud about. I hope you enjoy reading about its life as much as I enjoyed researching it.

Jill Scott

When General Manager Laurie Nicol asked me in December 2010 if I'd be interested in writing about the history of the Grand Central Hotel I was reluctant. Having worked for over forty years with *The Sunday Post* and recently retired, it was time for a break.

What I hadn't bargained for was not being ready to hang up the tools of my trade – an inquiring mind and a nosey nature that transposes thoughts into print. The other thing that attracted me was a love for the city I've lived and worked in all my life. Glasgow is full of charm, character and characters and 'the Grand Old Lady' which was the Central and now the Grand Central is up there with the best of them.

I refer to the hotel as a lady, a matriarch with the ability to draw you into her soul and regale you with tales of her past from deep within. Her history echoes throughout her expansive corridors, it emits from every one of her floors and it reverberates around her Grand Room of Glasgow.

Until August 2010 when the Central was in the process of getting her makeover and was no more than a building site, I'd only ever walked through her doors once and at that point she was a shadow of her former self. However, when Laurie said she'd fallen in love with 99 Gordon Street, I was able, like her, to see beyond the dust sheets, where an army of workers refurbished her after eighteen months of closure and over a decade of decay. Subconsciously I was hooked and once her glorious past was unveiled and the stories began to unfold it became apparent this was a very special place.

Who wouldn't be in awe at sitting where Sir Winston Churchill once dined, staying overnight in a room where Mae West once slept or wondering what it really was like that day in 1927 when John Logie Baird's first long-distance television transmission flickered to life on the fourth floor?

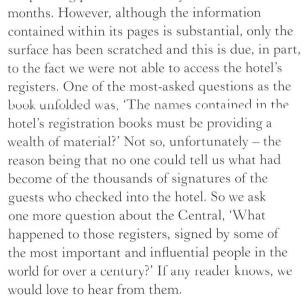

From beginning to end, the research, writing and editing of this book – prior to it rolling off the printing press – took many months. However, although the information contained within its pages is substantial, only the surface has been scratched and this is due, in part, to the fact we were not able to access the hotel's registers. One of the most-asked questions as the book unfolded was, 'The names contained in the hotel's registration books must be providing a wealth of material?' Not so, unfortunately – the reason being that no one could tell us what had become of the thousands of signatures of the guests who checked into the hotel. So we ask one more question about the Central, 'What happened to those registers, signed by some of the most important and influential people in the world for over a century?' If any reader knows, we would love to hear from them.

Thanks to the willingness of Principal Hayley's Chief Executive Officer Tony Troy to invest in a part of Glasgow's history and to everyone else who became involved in this project, like me you can now walk in the footsteps of the famous, live a little like they did and become part of the Central Hotel story.

Who knows, you too may fall in love with 'the Grand Dame of Gordon Street'.

Bill Hicks

Grand Central Hotel stands proud amongst its more modern neighbours on the corner of Gordon Street and Hope Street.

Central Hotel ~ Reborn

I n 1883 Queen Victoria had already been Queen for forty-six years, Liberal leader William Gladstone was serving his second term as Prime Minister, and Glasgow was still proud of getting the coat of arms which had been granted to the city in a patent by advocate George Burnett, the Lord Lyon in Edinburgh, on October 25, 1866. The words 'Let Glasgow Flourish' were officially adopted as the proper heraldic accompaniment to the coat of arms. And to flourish is exactly what the city sitting on the River Clyde was setting out to do.

Glasgow's coat of arms.

Glasgow people were not royalty or aristocrats and there was no castle or Royal residence to boast of – instead they were traders. The Clyde was their bargaining tool as the success of the Tobacco Lords in the 1700s showed. When the tobacco market disappeared after the American War of Independence, the city concentrated on importing cotton, sugar and rum. Chemical and soap factories and dye works sprang up near the river. These, in turn, were superseded by the development of shipbuilding, manufacturing and engineering.

All this meant a growing population for the city as people flocked to Glasgow from all over Scotland as well as from Ireland and England, seeking work and homes. In the census of April 1881, Glasgow's population stood at 511,415, having grown from the 147,023 recorded in 1821 when it was hailed as 'the Second City of the Empire'. (Glasgow's population in 2011 stands at around 593,000.)

Above: The landmark hanging clock in Glasgow Central Station.

Bottom: Grand Central staff await the arrival of guests at the re-opened hotel's first function.

The city was prospering, bustling with its own people, visiting businessmen and travellers. Train was the quickest and easiest way to journey between towns and cities, but, having arrived at their destination, travellers needed accommodation, preferably as near to the station as possible. The well-to-do of the city were also seeking elegant venues in which to hold lunches, parties, birthday celebrations and dances.

Fulfilling all these needs was the hotel which was officially opened on June 27, 1883 under the management of Mr Charles Lord. It had been built by a major player in the railway business, the Caledonian Railway Company, and was adjoining their Central Station which had opened four years previously.

The hotel was named, quite simply, the Central Station Hotel. Rising to five storeys and stretching along Gordon Street and down Hope Street, with a magnificent Swedish clock tower soaring into the sky at the corner of the two streets, it could house 420 guests plus all the servants (as they were called in Victorian times) required to see to their every need.

In 2013, it will be 130 years since the Central Hotel welcomed its first guests. In its lifetime it has seen the coronations of four monarchs and the abdication of a king. It has come through two World Wars, the Great Depression, played its part in the development of television, witnessed man not only flying to the moon but also walking on it and, in 1999, seen Scotland getting its own devolved Parliament nearly 300 years after the Acts of Union in 1706 and 1707.

There have been some bad times as well as good in the life of the hotel and from February 2009 it stood sad and silent for several months after the then owners, the Real Hotel Company, went into administration. Thankfully a new chapter soon dawned in June of the same year when the hotel was purchased by Principal Hayley and a £20-million refurbishment swung quickly into action.

Renamed the Grand Central, the hotel began to blossom once more when the first guests were greeted in September 2010, followed by a glittering official launch party on January 20, 2011. Built in the age of the steam train, the Grand Central has proved it is far from running out of steam. Just being inside this magnificent structure makes you want to step back in time to visit the era in which it was built and find out what went on within its walls all those years ago. So if you would like to find out more about the hotel's history and share in the memories of guests and staff over the years, let's start at the very beginning . . .

Left: The chandelier which is suspended through the Grand Central Hotel's main stairwell dazzles with hues of pink and purple. Cascading down a distance of over 70 ft (21.5 m), the chandelier was built in several sections while the whole staircase had to be encased in scaffolding in order to hang it and special steel beams installed to hold it in place.

Below, top: Detail of the fireplace in The Grand Room of Glasgow.

Below, middle: All set for dinner in The Grand Room.

Bottom: The lounge of the Robert Rowand Anderson Suite. The hotel also has the John F Kennedy Suite and the John Logie Baird Suite.

Opposite: The oak-panelled corridor leading to Champagne Central.

Below: The lounge of the John F Kennedy Suite.

Bottom: The corridor to The Grand Room of Glasgow, wide enough to leave plenty of room for ladies in ballgowns.

Right: The main staircase chandelier reflected in the baby grand piano.

Opposite page: Champagne Central lounge.

Champagne Central with stunning views over the Central Station concourse.

Above: Awash with colour, the Grand Room of Glasgow is ready for dinner.

Right: Detail of the elaborate gold-leaf-flecked wooden cornicing to be found fringing the Champagne Central bar.

Right: An executive suite bedroom.

Bottom right: Tempus Restaurant – formerly the Malmaison.

Below: Detail of the etched glass in the door of an executive meeting room.

Bottom: The Heritage Meeting Room ready for business.

CALEDONIA[N]
CENTRAL HO[TEL]

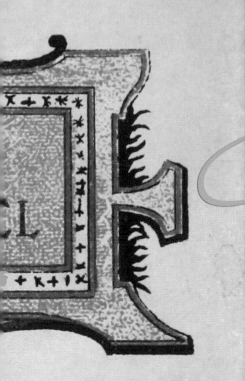

Glasgow

Hotel Manager

. Timbrell.

Detail of cover art from the
Caledonian Hotels Annual of 1892.

Glasgow and the Central Hotel

As the name denotes, the Central Hotel occupied the most central position in Glasgow on the corner of Hope Street and Gordon Street, two of the city's busiest thoroughfares. Gordon Street was named after Alexander Gordon who built a mansion there in 1804. Widely known as Alexander 'Picture' Gordon, he was noted as a collector of rare and valuable paintings. Hope Street was originally called Copenhagen Street but its name changed in recognition of the bravery displayed by Sir John Hope, Fourth Earl of Hopetoun in the Peninsular War of 1808–1814.

Detail of ironwork from the hotel's
Hope Street exterior.

In a city with the oldest Chamber of Commerce in the UK (founded in 1783 exactly 100 years before the Central was opened), the hotel was within a stone's throw of Waterloo Street Postal and Telegraph offices and five minutes' walk of the Royal Exchange and the Stock Exchange, making it an ideal place for businessmen to stay.

Lady guests could take a stroll round a fashion store. At the corner of Gordon Street and Renfield Street, just along from the hotel, was R W Forsyth which had opened in 1872 and, in Buchanan Street, Frasers had welcomed its first customers in 1849.

Guests could, if they wished, sit quietly in a reading room and catch up with the news – in 1883 the *Glasgow Herald* was in its 101st year, had twelve pages and cost 1d (one old penny). However, if they had more inquisitive minds, there was the largest reference library in Scotland (and later Europe) to browse through – the Mitchell Library. The library was a bequest from Stephen Mitchell, the owner of a wealthy tobacco business. It opened in 1877 in temporary premises at a corner of Ingram Street and Albion Street but moved because of the volume of people visiting. In 1891 the library moved to 21 Miller Street and finally to its present location in North Street/Kent Road in 1911. The Memorial Stone was laid in 1907 by Andrew Carnegie LLD, the great American benefactor of libraries.

The Central was the nearest first-class hotel to the Broomielaw Wharf where many river and sea steamers picked up their passengers for a trip 'doon the watter' including those belonging to Mr David MacBrayne whose offices were opposite the hotel. In 1889 Caledonian Railway formed the Caledonian Steam Packet Co. and became interlinked with MacBrayne's. In 1973 the company became known as Caledonian MacBrayne, a name recognised by us all today.

A Fireplace
in Coffee
Room

Victorian Railway Mania

The origins of the Central Station and the Central Hotel go back to the 1840s when speculative investment in railways for the Victorian middle classes was at its height. The Industrial Revolution demanded transporting goods by train which was faster than using horse-drawn carriages or barges on canals. Industry thought the extension of lines between major cities and towns vital to their development. Days out by the seaside, and visiting friends by train became popular pastimes for the Victorians.

Direct rail communication between Scotland and England had been talked about as early as 1833 and in 1845 the Caledonian Railway Act of 1845 authorised the Caledonian Railway Company to construct the final section (from Carlisle to Glasgow) of the first through railway from London to central Scotland. Buchanan Street Station, Caledonian Railway's first station in Glasgow, opened on November 1, 1849. It was initially the main terminus with all main-line traffic to and from the south concentrated there.

Caledonian Railway's main rival was the Glasgow and South Western Railway. Both companies were determined to beat the other in building a bridge across the Clyde in order to construct a station on the north side of the river nearer the business centre of the developing city. After many years of wrangling the G & SW Railway won the race and they opened St Enoch Station in 1876.

In 1875 Caledonian Railway was granted permission to build a four-track bridge across

the Clyde for the line from Bridge Street Station south of the river. Compensation to the Clyde Trustees for the loss of quay frontage alone cost the company £70,500. The contract to build the bridge went to Sir William Arrol, the well-respected Dalmarnock-based bridge-maker and head of Glasgow's most successful engineering company in the Victorian era.

The new line and its station north of the river – aptly called Central Station because it was central to everything – was officially opened on August 1, 1879. The occasion did not pass without fuss. A guest party of 150 gentlemen met at Bridge Street and were transported by train across the new bridge and over Argyle Street into Central Station.

There were a number of speeches including one congratulating Sir William Arrol on his successful completion of the viaduct across the river. Another mentioned the adjoining 'unfinished offices and a grand entrance to Gordon Street being shut off by boards closely joined together.' The 'unfinished offices' were never to be completed. Instead, a change of plans the following year led to the opening of a very grand and elegant hotel.

The New Central Hotel

Caledonian Railway's original plans had been to build a fine suite of new offices adjoining Central Station to have as the company headquarters as their old offices were no longer adequate for their staffing needs.

However, once again they were looking with envy at what the opposition was achieving. The St Enoch Hotel, built over the railway station entrance was officially opened on July 3, 1879 just a few weeks before the Central Station welcomed its first passengers. Described as the 'most imposing

Inset: 'Holidays on The Scottish Fiords' proclaims a Caledonian Railway brochure.

Opposite page, top, middle: Central Station and the Caledonian Railway office (as it was then planned to become) under construction.

Opposite page, bottom: Outfitter R W Forsyth open for business on the corner of Renfield Street and Gordon Street, circa 1916.

Above: The 1909 Caledonian Railway Company's Hotels brochure, the cover featuring the company's two flagship hotels: the Central of Glasgow, and the Princes Street Station Hotel, Edinburgh.

structure in Glasgow', it had 200 bedrooms, 20 public rooms and a staff of 80 men and women. It was the largest hotel in Scotland and classed as Glasgow's equivalent to the elegant and stylish St Pancras Hotel in London.

Caledonian Railway had planned to build a hotel on Hope Street just across the road but it made sense instead to have the hotel adjoining the station. Weary and hungry after a long journey, travellers could get off a train and go straight to their accommodation. So it came about that in October 1880 Caledonian Railway announced the conversion of the offices 'shut off by boards closely joined together' into a hotel.

It meant a large number of alterations for the architect, Sir Robert Rowand Anderson, whose original designs for the offices had been produced in 1877. Offices don't have ballrooms, dining rooms, writing rooms, family bedrooms or a magnificent 7 ft 8 in-wide staircase rising up through a clock tower!

So how did the hotel look when it was completed and ready to welcome guests? Here is how the main areas of the hotel are described in early promotional brochures:

Smoking Room

In the entrance hall the entire floor is laid out in marble mosaic. Here there are telephones, writing desks, leathern settees and lounges. There is an area where visitors' names are taken and rooms let.

The hall porters handle the letters, telegrams and parcels. Every hall porter

ought to be possessed of the patience of Job and the information of an encyclopaedia.

From the hall springs a magnificent staircase of white marble – broad in its extent and gentle in its gradient and rising to an immense height through five floors. In the evening when the electric light is in full glow, to view the scene from base to top is simply to be dazzled by its magnificence.

To the right on the entresol floor is the manager's office, the reading and writing rooms, the snug music room and the drawing room. The general coffee room is richly decorated in American walnut, ebony and dark mahogany and adjoining it is the ladies' coffee room.

The grand dining room has splendid dimensions. It is over 90 feet in length, 40 feet in breadth and 29 feet high. The decoration is rich and the magnificent walls are panelled to the height of 18 feet with oak and up to the roof is filled in with deep embossments of maroon and old gold. Twelve great columns and 10 pilasters of pale Giardino marble hold up the roof. The broad baronial fireplace is surmounted by a great carved mantel and blazonry of the Caledonian Arms.

At the other end is the musicians' gallery, projecting from its alcove and supported by green columns of Cippolini marble. Access to this gallery is on the first floor and the view from it on a great banquet night is of a brilliance not soon to be forgotten.

Coming out the dining room on the right is the general office, another writing room, a cloakroom, gentlemen's lavatories and the entrance to the elevators. These latter are very commodious and are constructed with all the most recent appliances against accident.

No money was spared to make the Central as palatial as possible. It had 390 bedrooms, 13 public rooms including billiard and smoke rooms, 10 private sitting rooms, 40 lavatories and 34 bathrooms. Unless you were in a suite, bedrooms with ensuite facilities were unheard of. Baths and

DINING ROOM, CALEDONIAN RAILWAY COMPANY'S CENTRAL STATION HOTEL - GLASGOW.

toilets had to be shared, usually by seven bedrooms. Once a guest had bathed, a maid would clean the bath before the next guest took one.

The most expensive rooms were those on the first floor – nearer the entrance hall if those newfangled things called elevators broke down and you had to walk.

To look after the guests there were 250 servants, most of whom lived in and had rooms on the top two floors of the hotel. They were continually in attendance for the guests' needs and could be called by the pressing of an electric-button in each room.

There was a passenger elevator on every floor with a service room adjoining. Every sitting room had a phone from which guests could call the hall porter or the waiter's pantry. In the front hall visitors could use an 'instrument' installed by the National Telephone Company to phone out.

Double-globe lights of thirty-two-candle power lit the rooms. The guest area was decorated with thick carpets by the likes of Axminster, Wilton and Brussels. The furniture in the public rooms was mahogany, oak and ebony wood and in the bedrooms American walnut and oak.

So how far would you have to dig into your bank balance to stay at the luxurious Central Hotel?

In 1912 the tariff for a suite – parlour, bedroom, bath and dressing room – was from 25s (shillings) a day. The table d'hôte dinner was 5s. If the Glasgow weather was a bit chilly then guests forked out 1s 6d for a day fire and 1s for an evening fire. A hot or cold bath (who would want one of those?) was 1s and a sponge bath in the bedroom cost 9d!

Above: The magnificent original Dining Room of Central Hotel in 1906 – now known as The Grand Room of Glasgow. Six of the free-standing pillars seen in the image were removed at a later stage, to leave only two pairs, one at either end of the room.

Inset: A hand-tinted postcard of the same scene allows an insight into the room's colour scheme.

The Architects

The architect given the task of designing the original Central Station and Central Hotel was Sir Robert Rowand Anderson. Born in April 1834, he had already established himself as one of Scotland's leading architects by the time he was commissioned to design the Caledonian Railway's new station in Glasgow. Other prominent examples of his work are Scotland's National Portrait Gallery in Edinburgh, Edinburgh University's McEwan Hall and the Medical School at Teviot Place, and Mount Stuart on the east coast of Rothesay, the family home of the Marquises of Bute and regarded as Britain's most outstanding Gothic mansion.

Rowand Anderson made a tour of London's railway terminals before beginning work on the plans for the station and the hotel. Several designs were considered but it was the early Renaissance version with Italian and French elements and a Scandinavian clock tower which was selected by the Caledonian Railway Board on May 1, 1877.

In 1902 Rowand Anderson was knighted for his services by King Edward VII and in 1916 he received the Royal Institute of British Architects (RIBA) gold medal which is given in recognition of a lifetime's contribution to architecture. Passionate about educating architects of the future, Sir Robert Rowand Anderson worked tirelessly for the professional representation of architects in Scotland. He was the first President

Opposite page: Pictured in 1906, above the fireplace of The Grand Room of Glasgow is the elaborate crest of the Caledonian Railway. Subsequently damaged in a fire during the 1970s, the crest still exists in an irreparable condition, behind a partition wall.

Above right: Rowand Anderson's imposing clock tower in a 17th-century Swedish style.

of the Institute of Scottish Architects but died in 1921, the year before the Institute was granted a Royal Charter and became the Royal Incorporation of Architects in Scotland.

By the turn of the century the ever-increasing number of passengers travelling through the station and the growth of the city of Glasgow in general meant extensions were needed for both station and hotel and this despite the fact that the station had already been extended in 1896 when the low level area was added.

Perthshire-born James Miller (1860–1947) was the architect selected for the task. He is noted for his many buildings in Glasgow and his Scottish railway stations. Miller had joined the Caledonian Railway Company's drawing office following his apprenticeship as an architect. He set up his own practice in 1892 but continued to do work for the Caledonian Railway. Miller won competitions to be the architect of both the Glasgow Royal Infirmary and the Glasgow International Exhibition of 1901.

His alteration plans for enlarging the Central Hotel included extending the hotel further down Hope Street to a height of seven floors. A billiard room and a lounge overlooking the station concourse were also included in the plans. Work began in 1901 and the hotel re-opened on April 15, 1907.

The total cost of the extension project was £179,793.61 with Miller's fee being a lump sum of £1,350.

Grahamston Village

The plan to build one of the largest and best railway stations in Scotland along with an adjoining hotel did not happen without protest and controversy because in order for the construction of the station and hotel to take place one of the least-known villages in Glasgow's history, Grahamston, had to be demolished.

commerce and industry. There were tradesmen of all kinds working there – from tailors and spinners to upholsterers and cabinet-makers – as well as a doctor, a teacher, a Post Office receiving house and a church – St Columba's Gaelic Church in Hope Street which could seat 1,500 people.

Alston Street also contained the first theatre in Glasgow, albeit just outside the city boundary

Above: View of Grahamston 1793. The theatre is in the tall building on the right.

Opposite page: Detail of a map of Grahamston village and Glasgow, circa 1809.

Below: Grant Arms and Duncan's Hotel are the only buildings from Grahamston Village still standing.

Grahamston was described as a rural village but it was not out in the country surrounded by fields. It lay just outside of Glasgow on the boundary which, at that time, ended at Union Street, and it extended westwards to Hope Street, covering the rectangular area from Gordon Street down to Argyle Street. This long-forgotten village had only one street – Alston Street – which ran north to south through its dwelling houses and businesses. First noted on maps of Glasgow around 1680, Grahamston became established in 1709 when John Graham II of Dougalston feued 6.5 acres of land from Campbell of Blythswood.

By the time the plans for Central Station and the Central Hotel were being drawn up, Grahamston was a bustling community with a mixed population of Islanders and Highlanders, and people from Fife, Dundee, Edinburgh, Ireland and England. They had all come to Glasgow to live and find work and Grahamston was rich with

because those who wanted to build it could not get anyone inside the boundary to feu or sell a piece of land on which to erect such 'a wicked place'. The influence of Calvinism was still strong and when Alston Street Theatre had its opening night on April 24, 1764, zealots disrupted the performance by setting fire to the stage and ransacking the premises. The theatre survived but only until May 1780 when it was gutted by fire.

With so much life going on in Grahamston the residents, naturally, were strongly opposed to Caledonian Railway's plans and of the 600 occupants of residential and commercial properties in Grahamston only 42 were in favour. Almost inevitably the day came which marked the beginning of the end for the village. On May 28, 1877 all the properties that stood from the Clydeside up to Gordon Street were put into the hands of a contractor by Caledonian Railway in order to create the building site that would make way for the construction of Central Station and its adjoining hotel.

The people of Grahamston did not make it easy for the contractor with some of them refusing to leave, and it took until the middle of July 1877 before labourers could start demolishing the properties. At the opening ceremony for Central Station the contractor said, 'It turned out a very difficult matter to get a beginning made.' On August 6 work was begun on the first pier at Broomielaw Street and when it was eventually finished there were thirty-seven piers built 30 ft apart from Clydeside to Gordon Street.

Pulling down the old buildings revealed some interesting things: an old Polytechnic, wells, the old theatre which was being used as a grain store, an old gas works which gave 'considerable annoyance and trouble' and an old sugar house which had collapsed in 1848 killing twelve men. A considerable number of subterranean passages came to light, all built and arched with brick about 4 ft wide and 4 ft high and all soon to lie beneath the new station's concourse and platforms and the hotel. In more recent years many have been bricked up, prompted by new regulations following the King's Cross London underground fire in 1987 which killed thirty-one people.

Some of Grahamston managed to survive – but not for long. Between 1901 and 1906 Central Station was doubled in size on the western side and the Central Hotel was considerably extended down Hope Street, sweeping away the buildings that stood there including St Columba's Gaelic Church. Today only two buildings remain from this long-lost village. One is the Rennie Mackintosh Hotel in Union Street. Originally called Duncan's, it was built between 1800 and 1802. The other is The Grant Arms on Argyle Street, erected around 1803–4 and built on the site of a brewery operated by William Buchanan in the early mid-1700s.

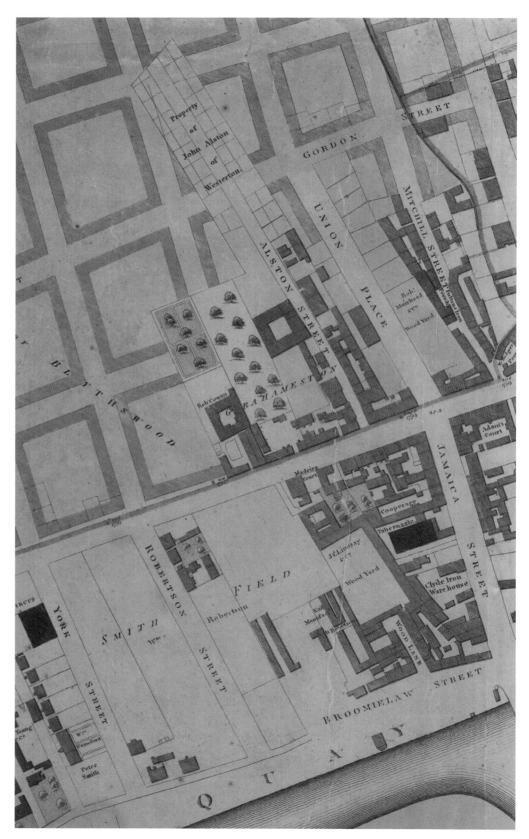

Below Stairs

The downstairs area of the Central Hotel was just as interesting as the upstairs. If any guests had ventured through a door or onto a stairwell meant only for hotel staff, they would have been astonished at what they found.

Behind the wainscot of the grand dining room, for example, ran a service corridor lined with polished marble with spotless white tiles on the walls.

There was a lift to take you down to the basement – a wonder-world of vast wine cellars, plate rooms, cutlery rooms and crystal rooms where glasses of every size and shape sparkled. There were pantries storing fruit and vegetables in the crispest condition and larders holding meat and game.

One area was as hot as the tropics with bakehouses whose bakers spent their days measuring, sifting, stirring and kneading to make the freshest of bread, scones, cakes and rolls not only for the

hotel guests, but also for the trains travelling from Central Station. A laundry and a drying room where it was like being in a Turkish bath contributed to the heat. At the other end of the temperature scale were ice-houses with arctic temperatures. The headquarters of this wonder-world were the kitchens with their 30 ft-high ceilings, long ranges, and array of copper pots, ovens and grills.

Move through an archway beyond the actual area of the hotel and calling a tradesman was never a problem, for here were the workshops of an army of electricians, engineers, plumbers, joiners, polishers, gilders, upholsterers and others, all on call round the clock to deal immediately with any maintenance problems.

Deep in the depths of the hotel, and breathing life into every corner of the building, was the machinery section. This was where great engines laboured night and day to ensure air, water, light, heat and power made their way through all the arteries of the vast hotel. Coal was dropped straight from hopper trucks on the railway overhead to the furnaces generating the steam that was converted by large machines into electricity that was led in turn by thick cables to a huge marble switchboard, 30 ft x 7 ft high, and finally distributed to both the station and the hotel.

The Heilanman's Umbrella

Not many bridges can lay claim to having a nickname but the glass-walled bridge carrying the railway over Arygle Street and into Central Station is one of them. Built in 1906, it is affectionately known by Glaswegians as 'the Heilanman's Umbrella' (the Highlander's Umbrella) – so called, because it was a meeting place on the Sabbath, which was their one free day, for the many Highlanders who lived in Glasgow and when it rained the bridge acted as an umbrella.

"DiDo" UMBRELLA CO., LTD.,
(GEORGE M'CULLOCH)
63 & 65 ARGYLL ARCADE (Argyle St. Entrance)
42 ARGYLL ARCADE (Buchanan St. Entrance)
208 & 212 ARGYLE STREET (Central Station)
Phone—CENTRAL 4393   ... GLASGOW
No.....   (over

It is estimated that some 30,000 Highlanders, who spoke Gaelic but did not speak English, came to Glasgow as a result of the Highland Clearances of the eighteenth and nineteenth centuries to seek work and for many of them the bridge was a convenient meeting place – near the centre of the city, the river and the station – where they could swop gossip and news of their homeland.

The bridge was designed by architect James Miller as part of his extension plans for both the hotel and the station – plans which were implemented under the supervision of Donald Matheson, Caledonian Railway's Engineer-in-Chief. Made out of riveted cast iron with tall multi-paned windows, the new Central Station Viaduct was built to run alongside the first bridge, giving a total of thirteen tracks into the station.

In 1998 the bridge was given a new look in a substantial refurbishment by Railtrack, (later Network Rail). The Venetian-style windows were reglazed and gold 'Central Station' lettering applied onto a green background. High-powered lighting and extractor fans were introduced under the bridge in a bid to make the environment more attractive to the retailers, whose shops line both sides, and their customers.

Top: The Heilanman's Umbrella, at the junction of Hope Street and Argyle Street.

Bottom: Central Station's ornate ironwork and glass canopy at the entrance.

Growth of the Central

The misfortune of two other venues in the city of Glasgow brought a certain amount of gain to the Central Hotel when it came to picking up business.

The magnificent structure of St Enoch Hotel, for example, had once been the Central's main rival. When built by the Glasgow and South Western Railway it was the largest hotel in Scotland in terms of its number of rooms. When St Enoch Station closed in 1966 and its rail traffic was transferred to Central Station it was at a massive cost to the hotel. It managed to stay open for another eight years but was eventually closed because it did not comply with fire regulations. It was demolished in 1975 despite protests over its architectural importance. Most of the shoppers in the St Enoch Centre today will not be aware of the elegance of the building which once stood there.

Facing onto the main entrance of Central Station

was the Grosvenor, built originally in 1861 as a commercial building by Alexander 'Greek' Thomson and his brother George. The warehouse-style building was rebuilt after it was almost destroyed by fire in 1864. After another fire in 1901 it was rebuilt again with a sumptuous banqueting hall suitable for dances, banquets and large functions. It had a magnificent marble staircase and marble pillars which made it a much sought after venue as everyone wanted their photograph taken there.

In 1907 the building was extended by the addition of upper floors topped by twin baroque domes which were occupied by the Grosvenor Restaurant, from which the building has taken its name. On the evening of April 1, 1970 the building was hit yet again by fire with much of it destroyed and the Central was inundated with people looking for alternative venues for their functions. The building was subsequently turned into the office building that stands today.

Below, left: The St Enoch Hotel in her prime.

Bottom, right: The Grosvenor Restaurant, directly opposite on Gordon Street, faced her rival the Central Hotel.

Above right: The 1906 Coffee Bar, beautifully appointed with gift boxes of chocolates available from the glass case.

Right: The original Lounge Bar, now the Regent Meeting Room, 1906.

Spanning Three Centuries
~ A Timeline of the Central Hotel

1842 Queen Street Station opens.

1849 Buchanan Street Station opens.

1876 St Enoch Station opens.

1877 Central Hotel designs are produced by architect Sir Robert Rowand Anderson initially as offices for the Caledonian Railway Company. Articles are published in the *Glasgow Herald* newspaper.

1879 Central Station opens.

1879 Glasgow and South Western Rail Company opens St Enoch Hotel.

1880 Alterations to the design and work to convert the Caledonian Railway's offices into what became the Central Hotel are announced. This includes a remodelling of the main entrance and the tower, which has already been partially constructed.

1883 The *Glasgow Herald* newspaper runs articles and carries an advertisement on the opening of the Central Hotel.

1884 Lighting in the Central Hotel is converted from gas to electricity.

1896 Glasgow Subway opens under private ownership.

1900 Plans are lodged by architect James Miller to extend the Central Hotel.

1901 Work commences to extend and enlarge Glasgow Central Station and Hotel.

1902 The James Miller designed extensions get under way.

1905 James Miller's designs for further alterations which include a billiard room and lounge overlooking Central Station's concourse are lodged and work begins the same year.

1906 The hotel extension which includes the ground-floor billiard room and restaurant are completed. The stairway to the entresol level has yet to be constructed.

1914 First World War begins.

1917 King George V comes to Glasgow by train and presents medals to members of the armed services on the Central Station concourse.

1918 First World War ends.

1919 Minor alterations for the Caledonian Railway Company are lodged, however there are no records of work ever taking place.

1920–1951 Minor work to various parts of the hotel take place over this period.

1922 The Subway is sold to Glasgow Corporation for £385,000.

1923 Hotel becomes part of London, Midland and Scottish Railway in a merger.

1927 John Logie Baird transmits the world's first long-distance television picture from London to the fourth floor of Central Hotel.

George V bridge over the Clyde is built, boosting the hotel's business from the south side of Glasgow. It's an easy journey with traffic coming up Oswald Street and then into Hope Street.

1933 The Subway changes from a cable-operated system to electrification and later becomes Glasgow Underground.

1939 Second World War begins. The Clyde-built Anchor-Donaldson liner, the *Athenia*, on her way to Canada with evacuees, is sunk by a U-boat with the loss of 112 lives.

1945 Second World War ends.

1948 The formation of British Transport Hotels with 44 hotels initially in the group.

1949 Glasgow's trolley buses begin service.

1952 A new entrance to the hotel is constructed on Hope Street for the Malmaison and La Fourchette Grill Bar. The entrance includes new canopies. The main dining room is also remodelled with the removal of several pillars and the Arran Room is created on the first floor.

1960–1970 The kitchen on the entresol floor is remodelled and bathroom alterations take place.

1962 Glasgow's tramcar system is scrapped. Diesel-powered buses had already been introduced.

1966 Buchanan Street and St Enoch Stations close as part of the renationalisation of the railway system after Dr Richard Beeching's report of 1963.

1967 Glasgow's last trolley bus makes its final appearance on city streets.

1970 The hotel is listed under Historic Scotland as a Grade A building.

1970–1974 Fire protection upgrades take place and a number of bedrooms are altered to accommodate en-suite bathrooms.

1971 Buchanan Street Station is demolished.

1977 Despite protests, the St Enoch Hotel is demolished along with St Enoch Station. Only the clock that was suspended from the roof survives and it now hangs in Cumbernauld town centre.

1982 Under privatisation implemented by the Conservatives the Central goes up for sale at the end of the year along with all the other BTH hotels.

1983 The Central is bought by the Virani Group

1983–1984 Work to add in further bathrooms and upgrade drainage in the levels of the hotel which contain the bedrooms takes place.

1984 The kitchen and basement areas are altered in La Fourchette.

1984 La Fourchette and the Malmaison are closed for remodelling as separate bar and dining rooms by Coleman Brothers Architects for international restaurant group, My Kinda Town, Ltd. The Hope Street entrance to La Fourchette is closed and the raised step, currently still in use, is inserted.

1984–1987 Work takes place over this period on the Kintyre Suite.

1987 Alterations take place at the Central Station concourse entrance of the hotel. The entresol floor is remodelled and redecorated by the Richmond Design Group which results in the lowering of the Grand Room

ceiling. Work is also carried out in other entresol rooms including folding screens in the dining room area. The ground floor reception area is remodelled by owners, Friendly Group Hotels.

1989 A new heating system to bedrooms on all levels is installed, as are new bathrooms and some rooms are subdivided to provide more bedroom capacity.

1991 A new leisure club opens in the basement area with an entrance from Hope Street and substantial changes are made to the original kitchens and staff areas.

2000–2009 The Black and White Club carry out extensive alterations to 50 Hope Street, the address of the now-closed Malmaison. Friendly Group Hotels redecorate the Gordon Street bedrooms and install partial air conditioning.

2009
(June) The Central Hotel is purchased by Principal Hayley, who carry out a £20-million refurbishment.

2010
(September) The Grand Central Hotel is open for business.

2011
(January) The Grand Central Hotel holds an official party to relaunch the hotel attended by First Minister Alex Salmond.

À la Carte

When the Caledonian Railway Company became part of London, Midland and Scottish Railway (LMS) in 1923, it brought two of the finest hotels in Scotland to the merger. As well as the Central Hotel, there was the Caledonian Hotel in Edinburgh which had opened in December 1903 and adjoined Princes Street Station. Caledonian Railway had been planning to build a third hotel in Gleneagles in Perthshire but the First World War delayed the project and the building of this world famous hotel was only completed by LMS in 1924, by which time they could boast of being the largest hotel-owning company in Europe. In 1947, a book published

ENTRESOL FLOOR
for the
MALMAISON RESTAURANT & FOYER
also for
AMERICAN BAR

A glass wall-sign from the past which was discovered in the hotel's attic.

The ornate hand-painted tin ceiling brings an air of grandeur to Deli Central, previously La Fourchette.

Above: The 1970s Malmaison menu depicting Napoleon and Josephine whose home outside Paris gave the famous restaurant its name.

by the LMS to celebrate Caledonian's centenary stated, 'The hotels are furnished and equipped in accordance with the best available standards, they offer rest and refreshment to a wide and ever-growing clientele.'

Back in 1923, when the merger took place, there was one man who was giving much thought to establishing an 'ever-growing clientele' in the hotels now under the LMS umbrella. His name was Arthur Towle and his title was Controller, LMS Hotel Services. At the time railway companies were looking at how they could maximise their custom with train travellers, especially once they had reached their destination. Arthur needed to look no further than his own family for advice. His father, Sir William Towle, had been behind the creation of many of the top British hotels in the nineteenth century. Arthur decided that the restaurants within LMS hotels needed to provide excellent food and service in order to boost business and he began by creating the Malmaison in the Central Hotel. The restaurant, which could be accessed from the hotel and by an entrance on Hope Street, served its first diners in 1927.

The name was not chosen for its translation from the French which means 'sick or bad house' – rather a strange choice for a restaurant aiming to win customers over with gastronomic delights – but for its link to one of the greatest love stories in history, that of Napoleon and Josephine Bonaparte and their association with the Château de Malmaison, a magnificent country house in a lovely setting about seven miles from the centre of Paris. Bought by Josephine in 1799 for her husband, it was the place where they felt most at home. Today, the château is open to visitors and is a popular venue for weddings.

The Malmaison followed the culinary practices of the great French master chef, Auguste Escoffier. Born in Provence in 1846, Escoffier is universally recognised as the finest chef of his time. At the age of thirteen he went to Nice to work in his uncle's restaurant and then moved on to restaurants in Paris, Switzerland, Monte Carlo and London, all the time picking up the skills which earned him the title of 'the King of chefs and the chef of Kings'.

He invented over 10,000 recipes with two of the most famous – Peach Melba and Melba Toast – named after the famous Australian soprano Dame Nellie Melba. Dame Nellie stayed at the Savoy in London when she was singing at Covent Garden and the Metropolitan Opera, and Escoffier created the recipes in her honour while working at the hotel. When Escoffier died in 1935 he left many legacies for generations of chefs to come, including the station-based brigade system used today in most professional kitchens.

When the Malmaison (or the Mal as it became affectionately known) was opened, Escoffier's practices were still relatively new but young and eager chefs wanted to learn his methods. Many young Scots headed south to London to work in the great hotels and restaurants which had already adopted Escoffier's methods before returning north of the border to work in places like Gleneagles, the Balmoral in Edinburgh or the Mal.

Glaswegians and visitors to the city fell in love with the Mal. The restaurant, with heavy red drapes over the windows facing onto Hope Street, was for special occasions, anniversaries and celebrations. Celebrities ate there – it was the place to see and be seen. While diners savoured every mouthful, live music played from a small balcony above them. Those with birthdays and anniversaries in August who wanted to eat in the Mal had to reschedule their diaries. For during August the Mal closed down while its staff were sent to Gleneagles or Turnberry to help out during the busiest time of the year for those establishments with golfers coming from all over the world to appreciate Scotland's courses, scenery and gastronomic delights.

For nearly sixty years the Mal ranked amongst the best restaurants in the country. Then, changing

Top left: The Malmaison in the 1970s. The rear wall shows the balcony from where musicians would entertain the diners.

Top right: Cover of a 1975 menu; and a 1978 set menu when the hotel held 'Une Saison Française' – a series of French evenings with a set meal held on certain Friday nights.

Left: Auguste Escoffier and his book which became the bible for chefs all over the world.

the malmaison restaurant

CARTE DU JOUR

HORS D'ŒUVRE
Hors d'Œuvre au Choix	4/6
Huîtres Natives (12)	18/6
Caviar Ocietrova Malassol	21/–
Foie Gras de Strasbourg	17/6
Jambon de Parme	9/6
Pamplemousse en Cocktail	3/–
Pâté Maison	4/6
Saumon Fumé	9/6
Crevettes Marie Rose	5/6
Truite Fumée	6/6
Mortadelle et Salami	7/6

POTAGES
Tortue Claire au Xérès	5/–
Consommé Madrilène en Gelée	3/–
Petite Marmite Henri IV	4/–
Crème Reine, Germiny	3/6
Velouté St. Germain, Portugaise	3/–
Bisque de Homard	5/–

ŒUFS
Brouillés, à la Turque, Chimay	4/6
Portugaise, Bénédictine, Meyerbeer	4/6
Omelettes Diverses	6/6

FARINEUX
Canelloni Gratinés	5/6
Spaghetti Bolognaise	5/6
Ravioli Italienne	5/6
Nouilles au Parmesan	5/6
Rizotto	5/6

POISSONS
Friture de Scampis	8/6
Gratin de Scampis Nantua	12/6
Blanchaille Diablée	5/6
Sole Colbert, Grillée, Francine	12/6
Filets de Sole Bonne Femme, Véronique, Bréval, St. Germain, Grimaldi, Dugléré	9/6
Truite Doria, au Bleu	9/6
Tronçon de Turbot Hollandaise	9/6
Homard Froid	13/6
Homard Thermidor, Cardinal	15/–
Homard Américaine (2)	25/–

ENTREES
Suprême de Volaille Maryland, Maréchal, Sous Cloche	14/6
Poulet Sauté aux Cèpes, en Curry, à la King	14/6
Poussin Farci Polonaise	14/6
Vol-au-Vent Toulousaine	9/6
Langue Braisée au Madère	9/6
Jambon aux Epinards	9/6
Caneton Bigarade	14/6
Ris de Veau Chasseur, Suédoise	12/6
Entrecôte Bercy	12/6
Côte de Veau Chez-soi, Milanaise Veaucresson	14/6
Côte d'Agneau Reforme, Clamart Zingara	12/6
Tournedos Rossini	17/6
Tournedos Meyerbeer, Helder	15/6
Coq au Vin (2)	30/–

LE DEJEUNER

17/–

Hors d'Oeuvre   Melon
Consommé en Gelée ou Trianon
Minestrone

———

Turbotin Grillé Maitre d'Hôtel

———

Gigot d'Agneau Sauce Menthe
Queue de Boeuf Charolaise
Vienna Steak Demi-Glace
Côte de Porc Grillé
ou Buffet Froid   Salade Verte
Jambon, Langue, Poulet
Côte de Boeuf Gigot d'Agneau
Veal & Ham Pie   Pressed Beef
Choux de Bruxelles,
Macédoine de Légumes
Pommes Rissolées, Sauté
Purée et Nouvelles

———

Pouding au Riz
Voiture de Patisseries   Salade de Fruits
Glace au Choix   Compôtes et Gâteaux

———

Fromage Assortis

2nd May 1959

A minimum charge of 14s. 6d.
per person is applicable in this Restaurant

Central Hotel Glasgow

CARTE DU JOUR

ROTIS
Carré d'Agneau (2)	22/6
Poulet Reine (4)	50/–
Poulet: Aile	14/6
Poussin Polonaise	14/6
Caneton d'Aylesbury Rôti Farci (4)	52/6
Gibier en Saison	

GRILLADES
Filet de Bœuf	14/6
Entrecôte Maitre d'Hôtel	12/6
Tournedos Béarnaise	13/6
Chump Chop	10/6
Côtelettes d'Agneau (2 pièces)	9/6
Chop d'Agneau Grillé	10/6
Mixed Grill	12/6
Poussin Diablé	14/6
Jambon	10/6

BUFFET
Poulet	13/6
Jambon d'York	12/6
Assiette Anglaise	10/6
Côte de Bœuf	10/6
Gigot d'Agneau	10/6
Langue Ecarlate	9/6
Suprême de Volaille Jeannette	14/6
Homard Froid, Sauce Mayonnaise	13/6

SALADES
Laitue, Panachée, Tomates, Française	3/6
Japonaise	4/–

LEGUMES
Petits Pois Frais au Beurre	3/–
Epinards au Velouté, en Branche	3/–
Haricots Verts Frais	3/6
Chou-fleur Hollandaise	3/–
Pommes Nouvelles, Sautées, Purées, Frites	2/–
Broccoli au Gratin	3/–
Endives au Jus	3/–

ENTREMETS
Soufflés Variés (2)	10/6
Pêche Cardinal	5/6
Poire Belle Hélène	5/6
Coupe Jacques	4/6
Ananas Frais	5/6
Compotes Assorties	4/6
Crème Caramel	3/–
Macédoine de Fruits Frais	4/6
Omelette Confiture	6/6
Crêpes au Citron	4/–
Petit Pot de Crème Chocolat, Vanille	2/6
Crème Fraîche	2/6
Fruits de Saison	

SAVOURIES
Croûte Malmaison, Derby, Midland	4/6
Canapé Ivanhoë, Galloise, Diane	3/6
Welsh Rarebit	4/6
Scotch Woodcock	4/6
Champignons sur Croûte	4/6
Fromages Assortis	3/–

eric   fraser

times and fortunes reduced bookings for those perfectly set tables, superb service and food to match. In December 1984 it was announced that the Mal at the Central was being converted into an American-style diner. The Malmaison had been consigned to the Central Hotel's history but not without leaving a lasting memory for all those who worked and dined there.

Page 6 EVENING TIMES Monday December 17, 1984

Mr Glasgow
LAST SUPPER AT THE MAL

THE MALMAISON at the Central Hotel, once Glasgow's premier restaurant, will serve its last supper in a few days' time.

Central Hotel manager John Peach tells me that the restaurant is a victim of its own reputation.

Although he has lately slashed prices in an attempt to attract fresh custom, the ploy has failed and the doors will close for the last time at the weekend.

He said: "People still think of the Malmaison as the kind of establishment where you can spend a week's wages without getting past the fish course. In fact we have been offering lunch from £9.50 for some time now, which is far from being expensive by city centre restaurant standards.

"Unfortunately the word does not appear to have got around and the Malmaison still has a reputation for high prices.

"Most of our customers come only on what they consider to be a special occasion and frankly there just aren't enough special occasions to keep us going. Some nights we serve only 10 to 15 meals and that is well short of break-even level."

Mr Peach admits, too, that the restaurant is far from being the establishment it was during its heyday in the 'fifties.

He said: "No money has been spent on the Malmaison in many years and that has become only too apparent. British Transport Hotels had plans to give it a facelift, but when the hotel's present owners, the Virani brothers, took over they were shelved. Since then there has not been the volume of business to justify a major investment programme."

Although the name Malmaison will pass into history at the weekend, plans have already been made for the building's future.

"We hope to start work straight away on converting the premises into a top class, Hollywood-style bar-restaurant," said Mr Peach. "We hope that it will be as exclusive a bar as the 'Mal' was a restaurant. If everything goes according to schedule, it should open in March.

"We have not decided on a name yet. All I can say for sure is that it will not be the Malmaison. We intend to make it clear that this is a completely new enterprise."

The changes contemplated will, however, receive close scrutiny from the Glasgow District Planning Department.

A spokesman said: "No formal planning application has yet been received for these alterations, but the Central Hotel is regarded as a building of architectural importance and any plan to alter either the interior or exterior will receive very close consideration."

Opposite page: Malmaison menu from May 1959. As well as the À La Carte, there was a set menu priced at 17s.

Above left: Executive Chef James Anderson working at the carvery.

Top right: Jacques Labat held high during his leaving party in 1977.

Left: How the *Evening Times* reported the final days of the Malmaison, December 1984.

The Malmaison Wine Club

Right: A tastevin was traditionally used by winemakers and sommeliers to judge the maturity and taste of a wine. Indented to reflect the colour and light, and small in size, they were sometimes worn round the neck or simply put back into a pocket after use. With many of them made out of solid silver, they are popular items for today's collectors of wine memorabilia.

Above: This elegant silver bar spoon belonged to Jack Donaldson who worked in the cocktail bar in the Malmaison during the 1960s. He had his initials inscribed on the end of the long spiral-handled small spoon which had a number of uses from stirring and layering drinks to fishing cherries out of a jar.

Right: A menu from a New Year's Eve Gala Dinner, 1976. A set menu of six courses plus coffee was £15.

The Malmaison's reputation for excellence extended further than its fine food. There was also the Malmaison Wine Club which sold its own label wine by mail order to discerning wine drinkers all over the country. Exactly how, and when, the club originated is unclear but its potential for development was apparent to Clive Coates, one of the world's leading wine authorities, when he joined British Transport Hotels (BTH) in 1975 as Executive Director, Wines and Spirits.

The wine club, named after the Central Hotel's restaurant originally catered in the main for retired directors of BTH and British Railways who could buy a fine Bordeaux at virtually cost price – a nice little perk! After discovering there was an interest in buying other BTH wines for home consumption and finding a file with the names of some 12,000 or so hotel customers, Clive dedicated some time to promoting the Malmaison Wine Club. The wine club had its own pink wine labels designed by up-and-coming designer Amanda Tatham.

Clive had worked for the Wine Society for six years so he knew how to sell by mail order and how to write up a wine so that it seemed irresistible. The club got great press coverage and within three years it was turning over £1 million a year and had a mailing list of nearly 10,000. To be a member all you had to do was place an order every year.

The number of hotels in the BTH group helped the club to grow. There were about thirty hotels at this time and holding wine weekends and wine-making dinners was a great way for them to attract more customers.

After the BTH hotels began to be sold off, the club started to flounder and within five years it had been closed down for good.

La Fourchette

The hotels and restaurants section in an official guide to Glasgow dating back to the 1920s lists the principal hotels of Glasgow as being 'the great houses connected with the three chief railway stations'. The three were, of course, Central Station Hotel, St Enoch Station Hotel and the North British Station Hotel in George Square.

Of the Central Station Hotel the guide says 'its grill room, entered from Hope Street, and the railway station, is one of the favourite luncheon rooms of the city business man.' The grill room was to become the Malmaison but alongside it another restaurant opened in 1952 when new entrance canopies were added in Hope Street leading to both it and the Malmaison. Given the name La Fourchette (it means 'fork' in French), it became a popular lunchtime eaterie for the city's busy business population.

La Fourchette had its own chef and catered for those looking for a less indulgent, less expensive and quicker meal. It closed along with the Malmaison and the two were remodelled as a separate bar and dining room.

Above: The Hope Street entrance to La Fourchette (now Deli Central).

Right: The colourful La Fourchette menu is from 1979 and what was on offer was in complete contrast to the fine French cuisine the Mal had on its menu. Leek and potato soup was 90p, turkey and ham salad £2.40 and a cheeseburger £2.65. A glass of cold milk was 27p and a roll and butter 19p.

La Fourchette
CENTRAL HOTEL GLASGOW

Malmaison Memories

Whether it was the rich pickings of the Malmaison or ensuring the pennies from the payphones were accounted for, nothing got past Tom Donnelly, Central Hotel Revenue Control Clerk between 1973 and 1977. However, not everyone took kindly to Tom's monetary inquisitions. One day Head Chef, Jacques Labat, whose mother sent his hats from France to ensure he had the highest available (the height of your hat apparently being a status symbol among chefs), followed Tom into the freezer. The money man wanted to quiz the Frenchman about the price of his lobsters. Chef Labat showed his displeasure at being questioned by walking out of the freezer and slamming the door firmly shut behind him – leaving Tom to ponder the errors of his ways. Fortunately someone released him before hypothermia set in.

Malmaison customers may remember the glass booth at one end of the high-class restaurant and might even recall Tom working there some evenings, writing every bill by hand, inclusive of service charge and VAT. Every item which had been handwritten into a balance sheet at the end of every night was cross-checked to ensure figures tallied and the books were in order.

Tom earned around £18 a week, which is why he could only gaze in awe when a guest ordered a jumbo prawn starter costing £3.60, but he does confess to 'acquiring' the odd one for a taste. If he worked late, Tom sometimes stayed in a hotel room, but if the hotel was full he would go up to the male staff quarters on the seventh floor. The sixth floor was for the female staff and although there was a communal area everyone had to be on their own floor by 10 pm. Anyone mixing with the opposite sex or breaking the curfew was dealt with by the feared head housekeeper, though given the size of the building and the fact she couldn't be everywhere at once, parties were aplenty. The social life among staff was good with bus trips, golf tournaments and other outings set up.

Above: Marianne Faithful was a guest.

Right: Sacha Distel loved staying in the hotel because of the fine French cuisine in the Malmaison.

Staff were always formally addressed by their title and surname. Tom had met and married Central Hotel wages clerk, Jacqueline Stuart, and even Jacqueline's boss, a Mrs Gillanders, or Mrs G as she was affectionately known, was always addressed by her boss as Mrs Gillanders. Many of the staff stayed in the Central Hotel for years, but it wasn't just staff who stayed for a long time – one woman lived in the hotel for over two years while her new home was built.

Although the hotel's star-studded heydays were drawing to a close by the 1970s some still stayed in the Central. Rod Stewart, Bryan Ferry, Marianne Faithful and Alice Cooper were guests, though Tom remembers being asked who 'she', meaning Alice, was. Sacha Distel also came and left his dinner jacket behind. It was a perfect fit for Tom who reckoned he would keep it for himself – until the French singing star sent someone around to retrieve it the next day.

❧ Before James Cairns began in the Central Hotel in 1976 he had two interviews (his father was asked to attend the first of these interviews by the manager). He was told he would have to spend three months each in La Fourchette, the Malmaison, housekeeping and the breakfast room, and was then advised to go home and think about accepting the job.

On his first day, he reported to Mr Fillipo in La Fourchette, a tall man who carried himself with confidence. With hair greased and combed back, he spoke with a soft, powerful Italian accent, using his hands to emphasise his words. James was introduced to the staff and instructed to shadow a young lady called Bonnie, who showed him the daily routine. He soon learned Mr Fillipo was not a man to be crossed. After being sent to fetch something for Mr Fillipo, James was asked by a customer for a cup of coffee and just as he was about to pour it out his irate boss grabbed the cup and threw it across the kitchen. James's philosophy of 'customer comes first' obviously didn't cut it with Mr Fillipo. James was told to go and never return. A sobbing James was sitting in the changing rooms, wondering how he would break the news of being sacked to his parents, when Bonnie informed him that Mr Fillipo wanted to see him. As he began to apologise to his boss, Mr Fillipo took a £10 note from his wallet, put it in James's top pocket and instructed him to go home, buy some ice cream and report next day when they could 'start again'.

James then began his three months under Mr Moretti in the Malmaison. Mr Moretti was extremely well dressed with very high standards which everyone was expected to maintain. He insisted on cleanliness and all the staff had to stand in a straight line facing forward with hands out in front, palms facing upwards. Mr Moretti would walk the line and inspect, checking that the men were clean shaven. He would then check uniforms which, for James was a white jacket with red epaulettes (commis waiter) and silver buttons buttoned up to the neck. This was complemented by black trousers, black highly polished shoes and a white apron which went down to just above the shoes. Any dirt or rips and you were told to change. If your shoes were unclean, you hadn't shaved properly or your nails had dirt under them you were told to sort it out and docked £5 for each offence from your tips.

There were four food stations and each staff member had four tables to look after. Each station consisted of a head waiter, chef de rang, a demi-chef de rang and commis waiter. The head waiter took the order and passed it to the chef de rang who read and handed it to the demi-chef de rang. He arranged the spotless cutlery for each course as well as instructing the commis to take the order to the downstairs kitchen. Commis waiters never went near any tables and were essentially runners. The main courses were on silver trays covered with silver cloches and if four main courses had to be taken upstairs they had to be balanced on top of each other.

Above: Rod Stewart

Below: Charlton Heston

Mr Moretti had the last say on whether or not a customer should be served if their attire did not meet the strict dress code. James recalls Charlton Heston entering the Malmaison with his family without a jacket and the barman, an elderly gent taking the film star aside. He then chose a jacket and matching tie from a rail kept specifically for such an occasion. Heston sat in an alcove on James's station, but he was not allowed to approach the film star's table. However, news quickly spread and some staff, especially the housekeeping females, infiltrated the little kitchen at the top of the stairs to peer through the round windows at the VIP. Prior to leaving Heston was asked by a thrilled Mr Moretti to sign a couple of menus which he did willingly.

A Lifetime of Service

Below: Banqueting Head Waiter Alfred Presswell (back row) with his staff.

Opposite, above: Presswell enjoying a jovial moment at work.

Opposite, below: A letter from The Chief Constables' (Scotland) Association thanking Alfred and his staff for a job well done.

Between 1936 and 1961 Central Hotel Banqueting Head Waiter, Alfred Presswell, crossed paths with some very important guests – Princess Margaret, Mae West and Sir Winston Churchill to name but a few – and when his son Brian arrived one day in the Grand Central to recount tales of his late father we sat up and took notice.

Every morning for twenty-five years Alfred would board the 7.18 am train from Hillington. Bedecked in his black Crombie coat and bowler hat, he cut quite a dash as he headed for his prestigious job. With his bow tie tied to perfection and not a hair out of place, he was known to polish even the insides of the soles of his shoes and his staff followed his example to the letter. Once his shift was over, Alfred would head home around four in the afternoon, though he'd return in the evening should his services be required for a large function or if important guests were in residence.

A fair and well-respected man, no matter how big the tips were – and some were very large – Alfred

always shared them evenly among his staff. Laurel and Hardy, Clement Atlee, Gracie Fields and singer Johnny Ray all parted with cash for tips, having received service par excellence from Alfred and his charges. If someone forgot to put their hand in their pocket though, Alfred wasn't averse to dropping a hint. 'Sorry I didn't see you before I left last night,' he would prompt, at which point the guest would dig deep, red-faced at their error. Discretion was very much part of his job, though Alfred did let out the odd snippet of gossip within the confines of his own four walls.

As for leftover food, it sometimes travelled home with Alfred, just like the cigars guests bought but didn't smoke. 'Well, they are paid for,' he would say. And, of course, one guest became world famous, not only for his war efforts, but for puffing the odd cigar or three. Sir Winston Churchill stayed in the Central Hotel on many an occasion and when Alfred got the chance he wasn't shy at asking (twice) for his autograph when the top Tory was in town. Known simply as

'Presswell', Churchill, Margaret Lockwood, Mae West, Richard Todd, Clement Atlee, Gracie Fields (pictured left), Nelson Eddy, Laurel and Hardy and singer Johnny Ray all signed Central Hotel menus for Alfred.

Alfred's son Brian can recall the buses lined up in Gordon Street to take Central staff and their families on the annual bus run. He also remembers the staff Christmas parties fondly and says adult members of staff danced the night away at the annual ball put on for them by the hotel owners.

Chief Constables' (Scotland) Association.

TR/NLCG.   *Chief Constable's Office,*
                            HAMILTON. 28th. January, 1955.

Dear Sir,

    I learned you were off duty when our proceedings finished yesterday. I wish to say that we appreciate what you did for the comfort of the Association, and I enclose our acknowledgment of this appreciation.

Yours faithfully,

Hon. Secretary.

Mr. Presswell,
Central Hotel,
Gordon Street,
GLASGOW.

Reminiscences of a Reverend

Below: The Reverend Tom Gillies with Chef John Fortune. The Reverend Tom Gillies was born in Broughty Ferry and moved to Dunoon when he was nine years old before taking up a post under the employment of British Rail in the Central Hotel. He worked there from 1949 until 1952. After leaving catering, Tom, who now lives in Hertfordshire, felt a calling to the ministry.

"I remember walking into the Central Hotel as a trainee Commis in the winter of 1949 as though it was yesterday. The kitchen was laid out in 'Escoffier' fashion, with each section run by a chef in charge of their own area. Four stoves were heated by a coke-burning fire with the flues running under your feet and each one was called a 'corner' where the four Chefs dealt with their own menu.

The servery of the lunch bar where Deli Central now sits was entered by a spiral staircase with no door so a draught screen cut it from view.

The Head Waiter of the Malmaison, Luigi, would sometimes appear with an à la carte order unknown to the chefs which caused a mad dash to have it prepared in the allotted twenty minutes. On one occasion a waitress returned with a portion of sauerkraut after a customer had complained that the cabbage was sour. Head Chef turned scarlet. 'And daunt the bloody fool know the cabbage should be sour?' he bellowed and his roar sent the complainer scarpering.

Rationing still existed in those days resulting in food being bought on the black market. Our charcoal grill should still have been decommissioned due to rationing but it was sizzling nicely, complete with steaks and chops. One of our Gorbals suppliers was once caught by the Ministry of Food. On finding our name on his books they made a friendly visit to inform Chef the supplier had been arrested.

Friendly visit became investigation, but the railway company had an arrangement whereby the manager denied all knowledge of any kitchen goings-on and sacked Chef who then moved to another company hotel, fines and removal expenses paid.

Then there was Vegetable Chef, caught by a land mine during the war and losing toes which made him tetchy. His speciality was sauté potatoes, but our new Head Chef had taken to helping himself to them. One day with his colander of potatoes on the hob, along came Head Chef, who popped two into his mouth. Suddenly, there was this great

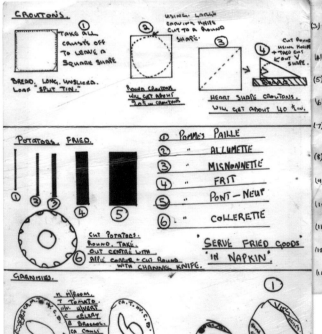

Left: Stephen Johnson started work in the Central as a Commis Chef in 1977 with a pay of £36.40 per week. Amongst his memorabilia of those days are the notes shown here, carefully detailed on the back of a lunch menu which was £4 for three courses. Stephen meticulously drew diagrams to show the different sizes of fried potatoes, croutons and exactly how a plate should be garnished! The other card details sixteen points of kitchen rules which had to be adhered to – from no boy questioning any of the Sous-Chefs' authority to not being allowed to talk to waiters or waitresses in the kitchen.

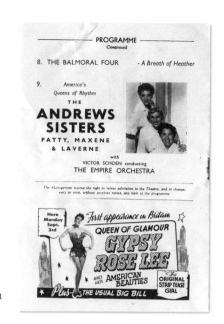

dish. He explained this was Chef's own make, then left and returned with the tinned variety. The Sisters said they'd wished they'd settled for Chef's soup and most of their tins returned across the Atlantic.

On another occasion a Canadian curling team gave their waiter a cardboard box, requesting that it be put in the chill. At dinner that night they asked for five steaks from their box.

'Yes sir,' replied the waiter, 'and what do you want done with the rest?'

'The rest of what?' they asked.

'The rest of what's in the box,' replied the waiter.

'There are only five steaks in the box,' they retorted.

The box contained five T-bone steaks so big that pre-war plates had to be fetched from the stores to accommodate them. The meat allowance then was two ounces per person and the only way to make a meat dish look good was to cut it extremely thinly so that it looked like a lot of meat. I can't remember how long it took me to stop cutting meat so sparingly.

Even though we didn't have modern health and safety rules the kitchen was run to extremely high standards of hygiene. Every hot plate gleamed, ovens and utensils were spotless and we had a never-ending host of happy customers. In fact, is that not the *raison d'être* of any kitchen? **99**

Left: The Andrews Sisters at the Central, 1951.

Above: The bill from their Empire appearance in August 1951.

groan and he rushed out, hand over mouth with the words, 'That'll teach you not to eat my bloody potatoes,' ringing in his ears. The potatoes had been coated in chilli powder.

Soup Chef didn't suffer fools either and on one occasion told his commis to put the ham in the boiler. Commis, a rather scrawny youth, complained the ham was too heavy. 'It's not too heavy for me,' scowled Soup Chef and catching Commis by the ankles and scruff of the neck, he plunked him into the boiler, leaving him to scream as he carried on preparing his veg.

Any Central story wouldn't be complete without a celebrity. American singing trio, the Andrews Sisters, arrived from the States laden with tinned goods after being warned that Britain was still starving after the war. One evening they asked if Soup Chef could warm two tins of minestrone. He hit the ceiling – then worked out a plan. He sent up two tureens of soup, one his own tasty concoction, the other containing the watery minestrone. The floor waiter went to the Sisters with Chef's soup, but after displaying it he apologised, saying he had brought the wrong

The People of Glasgow

Marilyn Gaya (front left)
attended a debutantes-style dance
in Central Hotel in 1954.

Back in the 1950s, Glasgow had its own version of the balls held during the London debutante season when young girls had the opportunity to seek out potential suitors. In 1954, when she was just sixteen, Marilyn Gaya's parents arranged for her to attend a debutantes-style dance held in the Central Hotel. She was one of a group of girls presented to the Lord Provost at the time, Thomas Archibald Kerr, and his wife, both pictured in the photo on the left. The two gentlemen on either side were Master of Ceremonies at the formal occasion.

Debutante Balls were started by George III back in 1780. For nearly two centuries young females were presented to the monarch at Buckingham Palace as a highlight of their 'coming out season'. The last one was held in 1958 after Prince Philip pointed out it was 'bloody daft' and no longer appropriate to the times being lived in.

Following the protocol of the debutante balls in London, all the girls had to wear long white dresses, and they were paired up with a pre-arranged young male partner for the dinner and dance. Marilyn (front row, far left in the picture) can still recall the excitement of the evening but it did not end in romance with her arranged partner for she never saw him again!

The Gaya family were from the south side of Glasgow where Marilyn's father, Philip, was an electrical engineering contractor. They were regular diners at the Malmaison, enjoying the excellent service provided by Head Waiter Luigi Balzaretti and his staff. Philip was a great dancer and he loved Latin American in particular. At functions in the hotel Marilyn often partnered him when her mother, Maidie, wanted to sit out a dance. One of their favourite bands was Kenny Ball and his Jazzmen. Marilyn met Danny Kaye in the Central, as well as Mario Lanza, the American tenor and Hollywood star of the late 1940s and 50s who came to Scotland to perform in January 1958.

Above: Kelvingrove Art Gallery and Museum, in Kelvingrove Park.

Right: A massive draw for tourists coming to Glasgow: the 1938 Empire Exhibition, held at Bellahouston Park.

🐾 The city of Glasgow has changed dramatically since the first guests – the ladies in bustle dresses and the men in lounge suits – entered the newly built Central Hotel in 1883 and gazed in amazement at its magnificent architecture and opulent decor.

With shipbuilding and other industries now depleted, what makes Glasgow continue to thrive 130 years on? Today the main sectors of the city's economy lie in areas like engineering, renewable energy, life sciences, banking and financial services and tourism, conferences and leisure. The Glasgow Chamber of Commerce, founded as a result of the tobacco trading industry in 1783, now has 1,800 member companies all working towards the development of business in the city.

Every day Central Station, the building of which sparked off the idea of an adjoining hotel, has 105,000 passengers coming and going from its fifteen platforms, providing a huge footfall past the doors of the hotel. They come to work and play, to enjoy the vibrancy of a city that offers designer shopping, restaurants, art, theatres and concerts, and clubs and casinos.

And Glasgow knows how to put on an unforgettable show.

In 1888, Queen Victoria officially opened Glasgow's newly built City Chambers and also visited the first of a number of exhibitions held by the city to showcase the arts, sciences and commerce. The Glasgow International Exhibition, held in Kelvingrove Park and chosen because Glasgow was then one of the country's leading manufacturing centres, attracted 5.7 million visitors and was followed by other major exhibitions in 1901, 1911 and 1938.

In more recent times, the hugely successful Glasgow Garden Festival in 1988 attracted 4.3 million visitors, and thanks to the

Commonwealth Games in 2014 the city is
gearing itself up for another major event, in
which the Grand Central is sure to play a part.
More than 6,000 of the world's top athletes from
seventy-one countries will be participating and
hundreds of thousands of visitors will come to
watch the events and see what the city of Glasgow
has to offer.

[SECRET.]

CALEDONIAN RAILWAY.

NOTICE OF ROYAL TRAINS

TO BE RUN ON

MONDAY, WEDNESDAY, and THURSDAY, the 17th, 19th, and 20th SEPTEMBER, 1917.

The Royal Trains will, on the several journeys, be under the charge of the Superintendent of the Line accompanied by the Locomotive Superintendent, and will depart from, pass, and arrive at the various Stations as shown in the Time Tables appended hereto.

A Pilot Engine in charge of an Inspector of the Locomotive Department, accompanied by a Superintendent of Way, will run 20 minutes in advance of each of the Royal Trains, and the Driver must regulate the speed in order that he may occupy the same time from Station to Station as the Royal Train, and uniformly maintain the interval of 20 minutes throughout the journeys.

The Locomotive Superintendent will select the Engines, and take every precaution to secure the most perfect class suited to the nature of the Train, so as to avoid any possibility of failure or delay; he will also select the Enginemen, both of the Pilot and the Royal Train, from the most steady and experienced Drivers, who know the road well.

The Up and Down Lines between Kelvin Bridge and Maryhill Junction and between Kirklee Junction and Bellshaugh Junction will, from midnight on Sunday, 16th, till 10.0 p.m. on Thursday, 20th September, be closed for all traffic, except the Royal Trains and Trains in connection therewith as mentioned in these Time Tables.

STANDARD INSTRUCTIONS for the WORKING of a ROYAL SPECIAL TRAIN.

1.—Artificers.—(a) The Royal Train must be accompanied by Artificers provided with all needful material and appliances. (The Company which owns the Stock forming the Royal Train will send Artificers with it throughout the journey.) The Examining Staff, where employed, must be on duty at Stations at which the Train will call, prepared to render assistance if required.

(b) The Carriages of the Royal Train must be specially examined before starting, and also at each place at which the Train is timed to call on the journey.

2.—Engine Head Signals.—The Engine of the Royal Train, and its Pilot, must carry Three White Discs by day, viz., one at the foot of the chimney, and one on each side of canopy. After dusk, and during foggy weather or falling snow, Three White Lights must be carried in the same position.

3.—Working and Other Special Notices.—The Enginemen and Guards of the Royal Train, before they commence the journey, must obtain and make themselves acquainted with all notices relating to the Line over which the Train will run, and any instructions which may be in force with respect to slackening speed owing to new works, relaying operations, junctions, &c., applicable to the route over which the Train will run, must be strictly observed.

4.—Telegraph Men Accompanying Royal Train.—Competent telegraph men, under the charge of the Telegraph Superintendent, will accompany the Royal Train with the necessary instruments and appliances by which communication can be at once established at any place in case of need. The Call Signal given from the Train in any case of emergency must be R.X. on a Needle Circuit, and one long ring on a Telephone Circuit.

5.—Starting of Royal Train.—The Signal for starting the Royal Train must be given in strict accordance with Rule 171 of the Book of Rules and Regulations, and care must be taken that the Royal Family and all the Members of the Suite have entered the Train, and that the examination of the Train has been completed before the Signal is given.

Above: Correspondence sent out to stations indicating the
disruption the Royal trains would bring.

Right: King George V and Queen Mary arriving at Glasgow
Central Station during their 1914 visit to Scotland, during
which they toured many of the Caledonian Railway
Company's stations around the country. Central Station was
set out in fine style, with glorious floral displays bedecking
the entire concourse and entrance ways. The top right image
shows part of Central Hotel just visible through the bunting,
above the main station entrance.

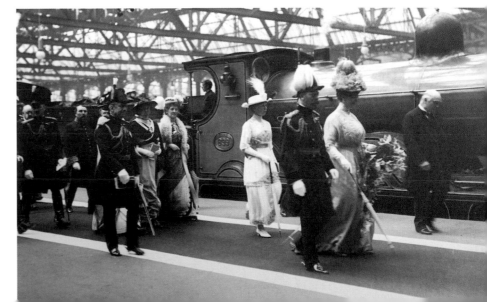

The Glasgow Fair

In the days when there was a mass exodus from the city for the Glasgow Fair, Central Station thronged with holidaymakers excited at the idea of a welcome break from routine – even bad weather could not dampen their spirits. Sunshine holidays abroad were still some way in the future and a trip to Blackpool or 'doon the watter' to Rothesay was more likely.

In the 1920s one of the most popular enterprises undertaken by the United Co operative Baking Society was the establishment of Roseland, a summer holiday camp at Rothesay. Available to all their members across Scotland and England, the accommodation was filled to capacity every year. In 1926, 2,500 campers from all over Scotland and England holidayed there, 380 of them during the Glasgow Fair period. They would have queued up to take the train from Central Station to Wemyss Bay then caught the ferry across to Rothesay and the camp. Roseland was, says an advert from the time, 'delightfully situated overlooking the perfect bay of this most charming and healthful of Scottish resorts.' For the princely sum of £2 6s 0d a family could have a week's stay in a cottage hut complete with a wash-hand basin.

In 1947 it was recorded that at peak holiday times, such as the Glasgow Fair, Central Station dealt with as many as 724 train arrivals and departures and approximately 120,000 passengers in a 24-hour period.

Above: The landmark painted wooden sign that hangs on the wall next to the entrance of Grand Central Hotel. The wording may have been updated since the 1940s (opposite page), but the message remains clear.
The sign is now protected from removal by Historic Scotland.

Opposite: Crowds queue in Gordon Street outside the booking office at Central Station, 1941.

It Could Happen To You

At a cocktail party held in the Central Hotel on September 29, 1955, football pools' winner, John Chalmers, was presented with a cheque for £38,583 by comedian Jimmy Logan. The event was organised by Vernon's Pools and John was accompanied by his brother and his very excited niece, seen here in the photograph with John (second from the left) and Jimmy Logan (on the right). John stayed calm throughout the event and happily allowed his cheque to be passed round the waitresses and others who were in attendance, all of whom who got a big thrill out of holding it.

EVENING TIMES   Thursday September 29, 1955   PAGE 11

SHOTTS MINER GETS £38,583 POOLS CHEQUE AT A PARTY

JOHN Chalmers, the 29-year-old Shotts miner who won £38,532 in Vernon's treble chance pool, was presented with his cheque in the Central Hotel.

Glasgow, this afternoon by comedian Jimmy Logan.

And John, surrounded by guests at a cocktail party given by Vernon's Pools, was the calmest man in the room.

As he chatted about his future plans or rather the fact that he hadn't made any yet – the cheque protruded casually from the top pocket of his jacket.

He gladly consented to pass the cheque round the gathering and waitresses and others got a big thrill out of holding it.

Will Try Again

John said – "I will go on trying the pools. There's always a second time."

He has left the pits for good, but apart from the fact that he will throw two 'do's' — one for his

workmates and the other for "the boys I go around with" he hasn't made up his mind yet what he's going to do.

John is unmarried, but he denied that he is a "confirmed bachelor."

Most Excited Guest

The most excited guest at the cocktail party was 12-year-old Anita Valerio, Mr Chalmers' niece, who is a pupil of Elmwood Convent School, Bothwell. She was playing in the school playground when John, on his way to the presentation, called to take her to the party.

John's brother, Bill, an insurance agent, also accompanied him to the Central Hotel.

John, who lives at 50 Lansdowne Crescent, Shotts, was a stripper at Stane Colliery, Shotts—and he'll be going along to-morrow to collect his last wages as a miner.

Mr John Chalmers (second from left), the Shotts miner who won £38,000 in a football pool, received his cheque at the Central Hotel to-day from Jimmy Logan (on right). Accompanying Mr Chalmers for the happy event was niece Anita Valerio and his brother Bill, also in our picture.

Right and below: In this iconic picture from the winter of 1957, it is December 27, there is a dusting of snow on the ground, and, with gloves in one hand, doorman Jimmy Cawley is hailing a taxi for a guest outside the Central Hotel's main door. The words 'carriage attendant' are embroidered round the lapels of the heavy mid-calf-length winter coat and 'Central Hotel' is round the peaked cap.

Both were much needed in order to keep warm, for Jimmy was not allowed to leave his post outside the entrance while on duty. He had to be there to welcome guests with a smile and see them safely on their way. If assistance was needed with luggage he pressed the large brass doorbell on the wall to the right of the door to summon a porter. His winter uniform was a heavy woollen dark-grey overcoat with maroon lapels worn over trousers with a stripe matching the colour of the lapels up the side and, during the summer, he wore a lighter version of the same. To finish off the look, peaked cap and gloves were included.

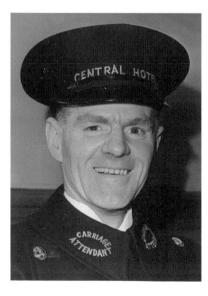

'The Perfect Building' – A Painting

In a whirlwind year since the opening of the Grand Central in September 2010, hotel manager Laurie Nicol has found time not only to get the Grand Central up and running but also to get married. The staff marked the occasion by presenting Laurie and her husband Paul Donaldson with a painting of the hotel by Glasgow-based freelance illustrator and artist Adrian B McMurchie.

Illustration by Adrian B McMurchie

Working mainly in watercolour and ink, Adrian likes architectural subjects and much of his work depicts buildings and landscapes. He says the Grand Central was the perfect building for him to paint as its Victorian design means there was plenty of detail to incorporate. He has depicted two aspects of the hotel, giving an indication of the vastness of the building.

The original painting was commissioned by *The Sunday Herald* when they used paintings by Adrian instead of photographs to illustrate their restaurant reviews. The hotel staff asked Adrian to produce a larger version of the painting for Laurie's present. Prints are available in a variety of sizes from Adrian.

Above left: September 1982, and after forty-four-and-a-half years of service, doorman Robert Marshall stands at the entrance of Central Hotel for the last time.

Left: Bellboy Andrew Lynch was a well-known figure from the hotel's front of house staff during the early 1980s.

The House of Fraser

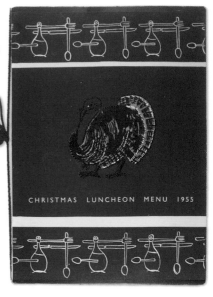

CHRISTMAS LUNCHEON MENU 1955

Although the Malmaison put the Central Hotel on the culinary map, the functions in the Grand Room of Glasgow and smaller rooms with names reflecting west of Scotland locations such as the Kintyre Suite, the Carradale Room and the Arran Suite, brought guests through the doors in large numbers.

There was also the hotel dining room – first thing in the morning it was not unusual to find a queue of briefcase-carrying gentleman waiting at its door. Straight off the sleeper from London, they were ready for breakfast before a day's business.

Excluding the restaurants, if every function room was full, the chefs and the banqueting staff could have had over 1,000 guests to cater for. Function rooms were booked for dinner-dances, AGMs, conferences, anniversary parties, bar mitzvahs, weddings, charity fundraisers and Burns Suppers. The Bridgeton Burns Club, founded in 1870 and one of the largest and oldest clubs of its kind, held their annual dinner in the hotel every year as did many of Glasgow's prominent businesses, from shipbuilders to plant hire companies.

In the Central Hotel, music through the years, in all its diversity, was supplied by a long list of resident bands and singers. Musical appreciation was behind the founding of Ye Cronies in 1877 – a gathering of Glasgow businessmen who met together, and still do, to celebrate the best in music and song by inviting artists along to entertain them. For many years the Central was their venue.

One of the hotel's longest associations was with the House of Fraser. The department store was started as a small drapery store at 8 Buchanan Street in 1849 by Hugh Fraser, who came from a farming background in Cardross, and Arthur James. A century later Hugh Fraser's grandson, also Hugh Fraser, hosted a glittering dinner in the Central Hotel to mark 100 years of trading. The proximity of the department store, which was to acquire some 200 shops over the years, to the Central Hotel led to strong business links between the two.

The House of Fraser became a major supplier to the hotel and, in turn, the company held their dinner-dances, staff Christmas parties and other functions at the Central. In 1957, to celebrate the twenty-first birthday of the founder's great-grandson, 'Mr Hugh' as he was known to staff, a five-course meal was served up in the hotel at a lunch held in his honour attended by the company's top executives.

His father became Lord Fraser of Allander in 1963 and, on his death three years later, young Hugh disclaimed his father's peerage, becoming known instead as Sir Hugh Fraser. He succeeded his father in the business but relinquished the chairmanship in 1981. The Al Fayed family purchased the House of Fraser in 1985 in a £615m deal.

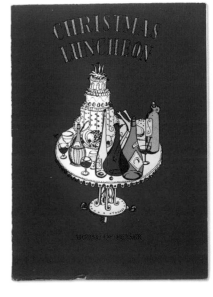

CHRISTMAS LUNCHEON
HOUSE OF FRASER

Hurrah! He's Twenty-one today

18th DECEMBER, 1957

Heartiest Congratulations and all good wishes to you Mr. Hugh.

Today, when you celebrate your 21st Birthday, marks a milestone in the history of the House of Fraser and we, the Managers and Executives, wish you health, happiness and every success in all your future undertakings. We offer you our loyal greetings.

Sir Hugh died of cancer in 1987 at the age of fifty but the legacy of the Fraser name lives on. In 1960, and in memory of his mother who died that year aged ninety-two, Lord Fraser of Allander established the Emily Fraser Foundation specifically to help people working in the retail trade. Around the same time the Hugh Fraser Foundation was also set up to support low-profile good causes mainly in the west of Scotland. The two foundations later merged and today Sir Hugh's daughter, Patricia, is one of the trustees of the Hugh Fraser Foundation which gives a million pounds a year to a wide range of projects from healthcare to museums. Patricia can remember dining with her father in the Malmaison as a teenager in her school uniform and attending staff Christmas parties in the hotel.

When Radio Clyde started participating in Cash for Kids in the early 1980s one of the first cheques received was presented to

them by Sir Hugh at the debut fundraiser held in the Central Hotel. Since then Radio Clyde has raised over £21 million and helped over 1.6 million of Scotland's most deprived children.

This spread: Menus and invitations from the many social functions held on behalf of The House of Fraser at Central Hotel over the decades.

Top left: 'Mr Hugh' (seated at the top table) in the Central during his 21st birthday celebration, 1957.

Sir Winston Churchill

Above: Sir Winston Churchill, and (inset) the Stone of Destiny.

Of all the famous people who crossed the threshold of 99 Gordon Street through the decades, none will surely be more recognisable than cigar-smoking Sir Winston Churchill. Born Winston Leonard Spencer-Churchill on November 30, 1874 in Oxfordshire, his list of political achievements are as vast, varied and interesting as the history of the Central Hotel itself.

On Friday, May 20, 1949 Unionists from John O' Groats to the Mull of Galloway turned out to greet Sir Winston and his wife Clementine in Glasgow. Over 2,000 followers lined Hope Street and Gordon Street, having waited for an hour before he made an appearance in the doorway of the Central Hotel. Churchill was in the city to give a speech to 22,000 supporters at Ibrox Stadium and he had made the hotel his headquarters. As the car carrying him moved away from the hotel, he rose to his feet and waved his hat. Two years later, almost to the day, on May 18, 1951 he returned. Churchill was in Glasgow to address the annual conference of the Scottish Unionist Association in the city's 4,000-seat Green's Playhouse. When he arrived at Central Station on this occasion he was met by more journalists, photographers, railway officials and porters than members of the public. Taking time to light his famous cigar before alighting from his train – which was two minutes early – he chatted to the small party of Scottish Unionist leaders as he walked briskly to the Central Hotel after being greeted by the station master. According to a report in the *Evening Times* newspaper the erected barriers were barely required for the handful of supporters heard to murmur, 'Good old Winnie'.

Britain had seen six years of socialist rule after Churchill lost the 1945 general election to Clement Atlee (born in 1883, the year the Central Hotel was opened). This was to change when Churchill was elected Prime Minister for the third time in October 1951. While in Glasgow during that May 1951 visit, he spent a short time with Lord Provost Sir Victor Warren. Sir Victor was a member of the now defunct Progressive Party, a political organisation based on an anti-Labour co-operation between Unionists, Scottish Liberals and Independents. That evening, although crowds of supporters had gathered to meet Churchill at Green's, his car had to divert into Renfield Lane under police escort so that he could be sneaked into the cinema by a side door. This was reportedly to avoid a group of Scottish Nationalist protesters demanding the return of the Stone of Destiny, but there may have been another reason. Cinema lovers – and Glaswegians loved their cinemas – had been forced to forgo a showing of the film Gilda, starring Rita Hayworth and Glenn Ford, which would have been showing at Green's that evening but for Churchill's visit.

War Years

During both World Wars the rail network and its stations with their adjoining hotels, including Central Station and the Central Hotel, had a huge role to play in terms of the movement around the country of troops, munitions, coal, steel and other vital commodities.

In the First World War one passenger who received a hero's welcome when he arrived at Central Station on July 31, 1915 was Private Henry May. He had won the Victoria Cross for bravery in action and was briefly carried shoulder high by the cheering crowd who had gathered to welcome him. On August 12, he travelled south to London from the same station to be presented with his VC by King George V in Buckingham Palace.

In 1917 King George V and Queen Mary came to Glasgow by train and presented medals to members of the armed services on the station concourse.

With so many men and women passing through its doors in the war years, the Central Hotel would have witnessed much of the sadness and fear that war brings, but sometimes there would also have been the joy of reunion and the safe homecoming of a loved one.

In the Second World War one of the first casualties of the war was a Glasgow ship, the Clyde-built Anchor-Donaldson liner, the *Athenia*, which was on her way to Canada with evacuees when she was sunk by a U-boat with the loss of 112 lives on September 3, 1939. Many Americans were on board and this act of war brought the man who was to be the youngest-ever elected President of the United States to the Central Hotel to meet survivors who had been brought back to Glasgow. John F Kennedy's father was the American Ambassador to Britain at the time and he and his son, John, lunched in the Court Lounge in the Central Hotel on their visit.

A year later surviving crewmen of the *San Demetrio*, which was built by the Blythswood Shipping Company at Scotstoun, were treated to a slap-up meal in the Central Hotel for the heroism they had shown after their ship was attacked in mid-Atlantic by the *Admiral Scheer* on November 5, 1940. The *San Demetrio* was carrying 12,000 tons of aviation fuel and her crew initially abandoned ship for fear

of an explosion but after being at sea for some time they re-boarded her, put out the fires and sailed her back to the Clyde. The crew were awarded a salvage claim of £14,000.

At this time the Central Hotel was part of the London, Midland and Scottish Railway group which had twenty-nine hotels open when the Second World War broke out. Some were immediately requisitioned for war service including the Central which was part-requisitioned. Restaurants were limited to a maximum charge of 5s per head and food rationing lasting until 1954. With the conscription of men and women, staffing problems were inevitable and older employees were brought in to try and keep the hotel open. Recovery from the war was slow and the prestigious standards of the Central's pre-war days were hard to maintain.

On October 1, 2006, the SSAFA (Soldiers, Sailors, Airmen and Families Association) held a dance in the Central Hotel to mark the 60th anniversary of the end of the Second World War and also the 120th anniversary of the charity which supports anyone who is, or has been, in the armed forces. The venue was chosen specially because it was one of the few hotels to survive in the city centre from war time. One hundred veterans were invited to come along with their wartime memories and to dance the night away to music supplied by legendary Glasgow band-leader Harry Margolis and his Big Band.

Every Armistice Day, November 11, a remembrance service is held on the concourse of Central Station to remember those who have died in conflict and the manager of the Grand Central Hotel is among those laying wreaths.

Top: John F Kennedy in 1947.

Above: The War Memorial at the entrance of Glasgow Central Station.

Inset: Harry Margolis.

Isa Blackburn was just sixteen when she joined the staff of the Central Hotel in May 1939, only a few months before the Second World War broke out. She was one of two employed in the printing room of the hotel to produce all the menus, not just for the Central but for other railway hotels such as St Enoch, Turnberry and Gleneagles. As most of the menus were in French the teenager thought it all very exotic – as were the places they were going to outside of Glasgow. She often wondered what Turnberry and Gleneagles were like.

Isa and her working companion, Mary Renfrew, had quite a lonely job working in a converted attic bedroom (in the staff quarters area on the seventh floor) that was fitted out with machinery that had to be turned by hand. They saw little of the hotel, apart from the door where they clocked in and the lift taking them up and down the seven storeys to the printing room, so they often left the door open so anyone passing could come in for a chat.

If a bride wanted a special menu with silver printing Isa had to visit a small room in the basement of the hotel where she poured silver powder over the lettering to make it look more elegant. It was a dusty task with the powder going everywhere. She wore a headscarf to protect her hair, and when she was finished a chef would bring her either ice cream or some milk to drink to clear the powder from her throat.

When the war started, Isa carried a gas mask at all times. Hotel staff had to carry out fire-watching duties and air-raid practices which could see them dashing from the top of the building to the basement. Isa can remember looking upwards at gas and water pipes and Mary saying if a bomb did fall on the Central maybe the basement wasn't the best place to be! Because of the war, most of the young male staff disappeared, their jobs taken either by women or older men.

When Mussolini declared war on Britain in June 1940 the effect on the Italian community living in Scotland was devastating – 4,000 or so Italians suddenly became the enemy and all male Italians between the ages of 16 and 70 were arrested almost immediately and interred. Isa can remember vans arriving to take away the Italians who worked in the hotel.

Her time in the Central Hotel instilled in Isa a love of crafts such as crochet which she still does today. Mary did beautiful crochet work and, in her spare time, she taught Isa. One of the first things she made was a dressing table set out of white crochet yarn (white was the only colour you could get during the war). She later dyed the dressing table set pink and still has it on display in her home near Gleneagles. For it was in Gleneagles, one of the places she had often dreamed about when printing off the Gleneagles Hotel menus, that the city girl ended up staying. After joining the Land Army when she was eighteen, she had first been assigned to a hostel in Crieff, before working on farms in the area where she eventually met farmer David Scougall. They were married in 1944 and raised a family of four.

She may have left her printing job behind all those years ago but Isa has maintained the skill of reading backwards!

🐾 In January 1943 Norway's King Haakon paid a visit to Glasgow. Regarded as one of the twentieth century's greatest Norwegians by his fellow citizens, he played a pivotal role in uniting his nation during its resistance to Nazi Germany's five-year long occupation of Norway during World War II. He had threatened abdication if his government co-operated with the invading Germans. As his train pulled into Central Station at 6 am that morning it was obvious that the city still slept since only a handful of Glaswegians turned out to greet him.

However, one man who did get out of his bed to welcome the king was Glasgow Lord Provost, John Biggar. The pair proceeded from the station and into the Central Hotel where King Haakon had breakfast and a chat with the Provost. Lunch at the City Chambers was next on the agenda. 'We want you, when you are in Glasgow, to feel at home and very welcome as a friend of Great Britain,' Provost Biggar informed him.

King Haakon responded by thanking the city for the very kind way it had looked after Norwegians who had been forced to take up home in Scotland during the war. 'We have only water to part us and as a naval man I say water links us,' he commented that day. He then went on to open the Norwegian Seaman's Club at 96 St Vincent Street, now a hairdressing and beauty salon, and attended a seaman's festival at the club that evening.

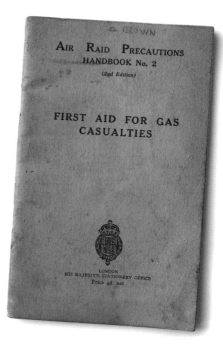

Above: A government wartime pamphlet detailing how to administer first aid to gas casualties.

Left: King Haakon of Norway, 1872–1957.

Below: Glasgow Lord Provost John Biggar.

Opposite page: A wartime scene as servicemen mingle with crowds of shoppers and workers at the corner of Gordon Street and Union Street.

'Putting You Through'

Right inset: Dame Clara Butt.

Below: A Royal Naval pendant – inscribed on the rear with the simple 'come alongside' – gifted to switchboard operator Margaret Innes.

As the Great War raged across Europe between 1914 and 1918, hundreds of thousands of military personnel passed through Central Station. Making their way to and from battle, it is not hard to imagine the scenes as loved ones bade them farewell, wondering if they would ever welcome them home. Many did return but with horrific injuries or suffering from the after-effects of being gassed on the killing fields of France and for all who returned there was the enduring trauma of their time in the trenches.

Yet, behind the substantial sandstone of the Central Hotel the military elite were living in the lap of luxury. Hotel staff attended to their every whim as their men slept on the concrete concourse of Central Station, kit bags under their heads, waiting for their trains.

During research for this book the story of one young woman emerged from those dark days. Margaret Innes (pictured left), was in her early twenties when she worked on the Central Hotel switchboard. Trained by the Post Office, she was ideal for the job – polite, courteous and discreet. Assets which, according to her daughter Joyce, caught the attention of many who passed through the hotel. Margaret regularly received flowers from visiting officers and many of her admirers came from the aristocracy but for the rest of her life she held on to one particular gift.

One day a young naval officer handed her a small, gold pendant consisting of three enamelled flags in a vertical line. On the back of the pendant was written 'Come alongside'. Her daughter Joyce is certain the young officer gave her mother the pendant as a memento of himself. She never did find out who he was, though she recalls her mother saying he must have survived the war as she had seen a photograph of him with his wife in the society section of a magazine. Why Margaret kept the pendant is a mystery, but it must have held a special place in her heart.

Margaret didn't receive gifts just from military personnel. One night a popular English contralto singer called Dame Clara Butt had been performing in Glasgow's St Andrews Halls. During World War I Dame Clara organised and sang in many concerts for service charities and in 1920 she was appointed Dame Commander of the Order of the British Empire (DBE). After her performance in St Andrews Halls, she returned that night to the Central Hotel where she was staying. On walking through the door she expressed concern at seeing such a young girl on the switchboard and handed Margaret a single rose from the bouquet she had received after her performance.

As for Margaret, who married in 1925, a future among the gentry was not to feature in her life. Concerned she was 'getting above herself working among those posh folk', her mother asked her to terminate her Central Hotel employment. And you didn't argue with Mum in those days. However, Margaret Innes never forgot her time on the switchboard, when she no doubt observed the lifestyle of the officers in the Central Hotel as their charges made their way to and from the battlefields from which thousands never returned.

The Steiner Hairdressing Salon

Steiner was a name that was legendary in hairdressing circles and if you had an appointment in their Glasgow salon, located inside the Central Hotel, then you knew you had made it in Glasgow society.

The history of the Steiner company goes back to 1901 when Henry Steiner created his own brand of apothecary items for both hair and skin. His son Herman opened his first salon in Mayfair in London in 1926 and he, in turn, created his own range of hair and personal beauty products. In 1947 he was granted a Royal Warrant after becoming Queen Mary's hairdresser. Six years later, in 1953, Steiner was asked by British Transport Hotels (BTH) to open a salon in the Midland Hotel in Manchester.

This was such a success with celebrities and fashionable wealthy Mancunians, that BTH asked the company to open hairdressing salons in the Queen's Hotel Birmingham (1954), Glasgow Central Hotel (1955), Gleneagles (1956), the North British and Caledonian Hotels in Edinburgh and the Queen's Hotel in Leeds (1957).

When talking in 1963 about his collection of 200 paintings, some of which he hung in his Central Hotel salon, he mentioned one painting he never displayed because it contained nude figures and 'Glasgow,' he said, 'couldn't take it.'

For seven years running, between 1959 and 1965, Herman Steiner took his family to Gleneagles at Easter when it opened for the season and they always stayed at the Central on their arrival in Scotland. His sons, Francis and Nicolas, and daughter, Michele, have happy memories of visits to the Central, recalling hot cross buns at breakfast on Good Friday morning. This meal was always taken in their parents' suite which had a piano in it, something that was really exciting for Francis who

was a budding pianist at the time and went on to become one half of the Rostal and Schaefer piano duo under his professional name of Paul Schaefer.

At around the same time Elizabeth Arden, who had a small beauty/hair salon on the old Queen Mary Cunard liner, were asked if they were interested in taking on salons in two large liner refurbishments. They were not interested but they recommended that Steiner be considered and the cruise-liner division which has become the focus of Steiner's business today was formed. Both the original *Queen Elizabeth* and also the *QE2* had Steiner salons.

A new Steiner salon opened in Gordon Street in June 1971 but the salon at the Central Hotel closed with the demise of BTH.

Right: Herman Steiner at work in his Mayfair salon in the 1950s

Art in the Dark

As the 1970s were drawing to a close, the sixth and seventh floors of the Central Hotel, once home to hundreds of live-in staff who had worked there over the decades, were closed off by its then owners, British Transport Hotels. However, after two decades of lying derelict, new life was breathed back into Floor Seven, albeit briefly, when in early 1998 the NVA arts organisation was commissioned to develop an art project by the 1999 City of Architecture and Design Festival Company. The company's name, NVA, is an acronym for nacionale vitae activa – a Roman phrase describing the right to influence public affairs

NVA was given a remit to create a spectacular and provocative artistic event with the emphasis on architecture and design. Their idea was to stage this event in the vicinity of Central Station and when the empty seventh floor atop the Central Hotel was discovered it was deemed perfect. Its dereliction and decaying interior offered a unique setting, allowing NVA Artistic Director Angus Farquhar and his artists to expose its dark mystique. Subtle lighting and sound was installed and performers brought in to act as ghostly figures. The plan was to evoke the deep and darker senses of visitors and where better to do it than inside a once-thriving, but now-abandoned part of a Victorian building. Between May 28 and June 6, 1999, audiences, if they dared, were invited to view the art project – ironically called 'Grand Central' – between the darkened hours of 11.00 pm and 2.30 am.

Having been the performing capital of Europe in days gone by, Glasgow has a great sense of theatre and one man who joined in the 'Grand Central' shenanigans was Walter Frintrop. A film extra for over twenty-seven years, Walter, who claims never to have shaved in his life, was the first fright – sorry, sight – visitors happened upon after parting with their £4. Dressed as a concierge in red waistcoat, black trousers and sporting his trademark beard, which has helped him land parts in *Highlander* alongside Sean Connery, STV's *Taggart* and regular appearances in the BBC's *River City*, he was a macabre sight on the hotel's seventh floor.

'There are rooms to the right of you and rooms to the left of you,' was all his deep voice spookily uttered to those who'd no idea what they'd let themselves in for. Even when a couple of young girls asked directions to the nearest toilet all he chillingly replied was, 'There are rooms to the right of you and rooms to the left of you.'

Other than a chuckle, as the young girls screamed their way down the stairs and back to the sanctuary of the living, not another sound came from Walter for nine nights.

Bottom right: Walter Frintrop in his spooky role.

Below: The NVA's event programme.

And screaming was the order of the night as the dismal corridors and rooms bewitched its unsuspecting guests. In one darkened room there was a door in the distance, ajar with light emitting from its other side. It drew people towards it, until floorboards began creaking and the door slammed shut, sending them scurrying back out. There was a room full of sinks complete with clanking pipes, a live eel swimming around a glass tank in the semi-dark, a TV with a picture showing someone on the roof (although in reality no one was there), and a burnt-out room looking as if it had been destroyed by fire. There was also the eerie 'razor room', a cupboard-like space with hundreds of old-fashioned razor blades half-embedded in its walls and ceiling.

Hoards headed to the seventh floor of the Central Hotel to experience for themselves this unique and provocative event. The artists have long since moved on to many other projects and Walter went on to play further roles in BBC's *Monarch Of The Glen* and *Rockface*. When asked if he never got just a tiny bit scared on the seventh floor of an evening, he replied in his deep voice, 'Listen, son, I've walked through cemeteries at night,' and without another word his ghostly apparition (long since gone after the hotel's £20-million refurbishment) disappeared!

Left: The lurid 'Razor Room'.

Above: Enigmatic messages on mirrors, ghostly apparitions and decrepit furnishings made up the NVA's art in the dark.

M S.   THE CENTRAL STATION HOTEL, GLASGOW

Wish You Were Here?

Whether sending a short letter to family back home or a request for a meeting with a business colleague, writing was the main way of communicating in the Central Hotel's early days. In addition to writing desks in the reception area, the Central had several designated writing rooms for guests to use for the purposes of putting pen to paper.

Reflecting the formality of the late Victorian period, one room was for ladies only. Its furnishings were comfortable with small tables and chairs dotted around a cosy room where a fire burned brightly. In contrast the writing rooms used by the gentlemen were business-like with one wall divided into booth-like sections for privacy. Posting of the completed correspondence required little effort. The sender did not even have to leave the hotel, for on every floor there was a GPO letterbox with frequent collections.

Guests were encouraged to use the writing rooms for creating their invitations, thank-you letters, poems or billets-doux in elegant writing. The writing rooms made housekeeping sense in terms of damage limitation since black ink from dripping nibs or spilt ink pots left unsightly and permanent stains on furnishings.

The Central had been open more than a decade before the pictorial card that we know as a postcard was an acceptable alternative to a sheet of writing paper enclosed in a carefully sealed envelope. In the United States the sending of cards through the post was permitted as far back as 1867 but it was not until late 1894 they were authorised in Britain, a move which sparked off a growth in postcard traffic as a cheap and speedy

means of communication. The posted card could sometimes arrive at its destination later the same day and prior to June 3, 1918 the inland postal rate for postcards was only half an old penny (½d). After that it rose to one old penny (1d). In November 1899, the 5½ in x 3½ in card was authorised and it has remained the most popular size of card to this day.

The five postcards shown here all fit these dimensions and, at first glance, all look very similar as each shows the same view of the hotel but the written words and the date of sending each tell a different story. The three oldest have 'Caledonian Railway Company's Central Station Hotel, Glasgow' printed on the front indicating they were pre-1923, the year in which the company merged with other railway companies to form the London, Midland and Scottish Railway.

Of these three earlier postcards, one bears a message on the front saying, 'This is where Papa is staying. Love and a kiss from Papa.' A clue to the destination of Papa's card is in the date – 11/16/05. It is written in the American style of putting month first and Papa's card is going all the way to Brooklyn, New York. For this service he has paid twice the ½d rate to send a postcard home to his beloved daughter. But how excited she must have been when she saw what a grand place Papa was staying in!

Another of these cards is dated a year earlier than Papa's, November 23, 1904. Its destination is East

Opposite: A detail of a rare colour postcard of Central Hotel, dated May 1925.

Above: 'Papa' has written the name and address right across the back of the card even though there is a dividing line down the middle. The divided back on postcards was not acceptable until 1902 in Britain. Before then the whole of one side had to be given over to the address, with pictures or messages, or both, displayed on the front.

Molesey, near London and, oh, the intrigue in the simple message 'You will remember this hotel, Yours, Ronald.' Was it a reminder of a romantic liaison, a family reunion, or where a couple spent a night of luxury, before embarking on a Clyde-based steamer to sail up the west coast on holiday?

Caledonian Railway Company's Central Station Hotel, Glasgow.

The postcard sent to Southampton from Glasgow in July 1904, reads, 'Have just enjoyed a great breakfast and feel much better. I am not staying at this hotel.' More intrigue. Did the sender breakfast in the hotel or simply like the building enough from the outside to buy a postcard of it?

Winging its way across the Atlantic for 1½d in June 1925 was the postcard in colour (see page 70). Miss Crotchett penned her message to Mrs Beard in Kansas saying, 'I sure am having a lovely trip. I like Scotland better than Ireland or England. Sure enjoyed the ocean trip a lot. Only sick a little part of the day.' One of the reasons why Miss Crotchett probably embarked on such a lengthy journey to the UK at this time was to take in the British Empire Exhibition opened by George V at Wembley on April 23, 1924. Running until 1925, at the time it was the largest exhibition staged anywhere in the world, attracting 27 million visitors. Miss Crotchett's postcard has a commemorative marking of the exhibition on the back.

Right: Sophie Tucker and one of her many records.

In July 1934, Sophie Tucker, the Russian/Ukrainian singer and actress sat down in the Central and exercised a little bit of self-publicity in the penning of a postcard to a friend in Dudley, West Midlands. 'Just to let you know my new Parlophone records are just out,' is all she says. The handwriting is flamboyant, just like Sophie's life.

Born in 1884, she was just a toddler when her Jewish parents fled Russia and settled in Connecticut where

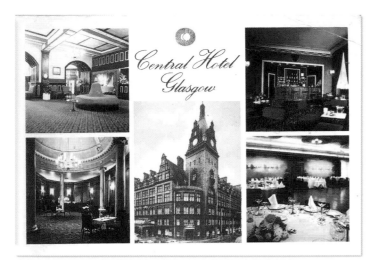

Christmas Cards

In the same year that Sophie Tucker wowed audiences in the UK for the first time, the General Manager of the Central Hotel, Mr Alex C Dickson, sent out his annual Christmas card. A small, simple card by today's standards, with only a robin and holly on the front, it reflects the sincerity attached to seasonal greetings cards of the period. Christmas cards were first marketed in the UK in 1846 and, like the first Christmas tree erected in a Royal residence (in Windsor Castle in 1841), sending Christmas cards was a tradition introduced by Queen Victoria's husband, the German-born Prince Albert. The three earlier cards sent by Alex Dickson shown here bear the same formal sentiments. In all four of the cards the greeting and name have been printed, saving Mr Dickson from having to write his name on each one.

they opened a restaurant. It was much used by vaudeville entertainers and young Sophie was smitten. She moved to New York at the age of eighteen to pursue a singing and acting career and managed to break into vaudeville in 1906. She landed a job with the famous Ziegfeld Follies in 1909 and was the headline act by 1911.

The 1920s brought hits including her best-known one – 'I'm the Last of the Red Hot Mamas'. In 1922 she ventured to the UK for the first of many trips, first of all to London and then performing to full houses in theatres in Manchester, Liverpool and Glasgow where she appeared at the Empire and stayed in the Central. She trod the boards right up until her death in 1966 and famous quotes from her reflected her larger-than-life personality. Here is one of the best known:

From birth to 18, a girl needs good parents.
From 18–35, she needs good looks.
From 35–55, she needs a good personality.
From 55 on, she needs good cash.

Top: An official British Transport Hotels postcard produced during the 1970s.

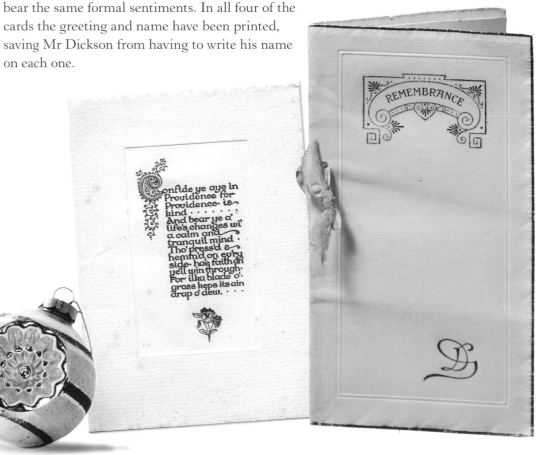

Honours, Landmarks and Launches

Above: The souvenir reproduction of the Caledonian's 1898 brochure.

Right: The Caledonian *Railway Annual*, Christmas 1909.

In 1897 there was plenty for Caledonian Railway to celebrate when company General Manager James Thompson received a knighthood – thought to be the first railwayman in Scotland ever to receive such an honour. To mark this very special occasion a celebratory dinner was held in the Central Hotel on July 12, 1897. A special souvenir cover in honour of the achievement was on the hotel's 1898 brochure, with visitors invited to accept a copy as a keepsake.

Sir James started off his life with the Caledonian Railway Company in 1848 as an office boy and rose through the ranks to become General Goods Manager in 1870 and then General Manager in 1882.

Caledonian Railway were well known for their printed works. Among these were an in-depth annual brochure for the Central Hotel and a number of slim paperback guides with titles such as Scotland for the Holidays and Holiday on Scottish Fiords. The guides informed tourists about the excursions they could undertake, especially on the west coast of Scotland where trains were linked up with the ten steamers accrued by the Caledonian Steam Packet Company by the turn of the century. In December 1909 Caledonian produced what is thought to be the only edition of a Christmas *Railway Annual*, described at a recent auction as 'an in-house magazine type of publication'.

❧ The Grand Central, itself a landmark, may no longer have a doorman on duty but just yards from the front entrance the bronze sculpture called Citizen Firefighter stands on guard. The statue, created by Kenny Hunter, one of Scotland's foremost sculptors, was unveiled on June 17, 2001 as a new millennium tribute to Strathclyde Fire and Rescue firefighters, both past and present, for their service to the community.

It was always intended for Citizen Firefighter to stand in a public thoroughfare and the location outside the hotel and station was chosen because of the volume of people passing on a daily basis.

Before long the sculpture had become a landmark and a meeting place for both locals and visitors to the city. The statue's presence became even more significant when, only three months after the unveiling, so many firefighters lost their lives in the terrorist attacks on the Twin Towers in New York. Flowers and tributes were left at Citizen Firefighter's feet and a ceremony to commemorate the 343 firemen who died on 9/11 was held in October 2001. On the tenth anniversary of those tragic events in New York, Citizen Firefighter was once again the focal point for a remembrance ceremony.

❧ Glasgow of old is synonymous with shipbuilding and for many years the Fairfield Shipyard and Engineering Company in Govan had a long association with the Central Hotel. Whenever a ship was launched on the River Clyde, dignitaries, directors and senior staff would mark the event with either a lunch or evening dinner in the hotel.

The Central was the main hotel for the functions of many Clyde shipyards and people from as far afield as Canada, the United States, Turkey and Israel would attend. In terms of the cost of building a ship, holding such an event was a small part of the budget and whoever organised these functions would be given a choice of excellent menus from which to choose the food for their lunch or dinner.

Between 1960 and 1966 the job of organising functions for the Fairfield launches fell to Ian Grant, who was once asked by a guest if it was all right to order up cigars as an after-dinner treat. (Fine to fill what is now the Grand Room of Glasgow with cigar smoke back then, but try it now and you would get short shrift.) 'Posh' was the name of the game in the Central Hotel, of course, and on another occasion one guest asked a waiter how to eat the asparagus tips with butter that he had just been served. 'Just hang back and watch another table,' was the diplomatic reply.

Over the years and up until the mid-1970s, all the main guests were taken from the Fairfield shipyard to the Central Hotel for their celebratory meal and according to Ian not a hitch in the proceedings ever took place. Very few launches now take place on the Clyde but thankfully the Grand Central is assured of a brighter future than Scottish shipbuilding.

Glasgow's Leading Hotels

THE CENTRAL

and its Malmaison Restaurant, famous for fine cuisine, and La Fourchette for quick meals.

Telephone: Central 9680

★

THE
NORTH BRITISH

adjacent to Queen Street Station.

Telephone: Douglas 6711

★

THE ST. ENOCH

adjacent to St. Enoch Station.

Telephone: Central 7033

★

The Resident Managers will be happy to give full details.

Left: The Citizen Firefighter bronze statue.

Above: An advert from Fairfield's 1960 Centenary Edition of the *Journal of Commerce.*

Top: The skyline of Glasgow's shipyards.

Central Hotel Weddings

Society has changed a lot since the Central Hotel first opened but one thing we all still love doing is going to a wedding. It is a happy occasion, a time of celebration and excitement, with maybe a few tears for the past and some fears for the future. Through the years, thousands of confetti-covered newlyweds have passed through the Central's doors. All of them can no doubt recall something memorable about the day they took their wedding vows, whether it was the best man who forgot the ring, the amazing dress worn by the bride or the honeymoon which had to be cancelled because one of the newlyweds took ill. Here are some of their stories.

Honeymoon Baggage

Right: Nan and George Grimstead's official wedding photograph 1952.

Far right and opposite page: The final bill for their stay showing the very expensive telephone call and a guest card showing their room number.

As a special treat many young couples chose to spend the first night of their married life in the Central Hotel, savouring together its luxurious surroundings, and so it was with Nan and George Grimstead. Their marriage in St Margaret's Church in Renfrew on September 26, 1952 was followed by a steak-pie meal with their guests at the reception in Paisley Co-operative Tea Rooms, a popular venue then for wedding functions.

For their honeymoon they were heading south to stay with relations in Seascale in Cumbria and, as their train was leaving from Central Station the morning after the wedding, they decided to mark their first night together as man and wife by staying in the Central Hotel. During the wedding preparations they had come into the city centre to make a booking in person, only to be told they had to put their request for a room in writing, which Nan duly did.

After a happy send-off by their guests the young couple travelled by taxi into the city centre, trying to hide the fact they were newlyweds by asking the driver to stop so that they could get rid of all the confetti in their hair and clothing.

Nan had never been in a hotel before and this one was very

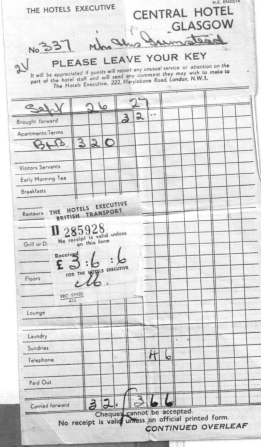

grand. Along corridors of lush carpet and décor, a uniformed porter showed them to Room 337 which came, not with the ensuite facilities expected today, but a chamber pot in a bedside cabinet! Throughout the evening a cultured male voice could be heard announcing train departures and arrivals over the tannoy in Central Station.

Following a hearty breakfast the next morning the Grimsteads prepared to settle their bill and got a shock. The cost of one night came to £3 6s 6d – half of George's weekly wage as an engineer. The cost of bed and breakfast was £3 2s 0d and the additional 4s 6d had come about because the novelty factor of a phone in the bedroom had led to George phoning down to the station to verify the time of their train.

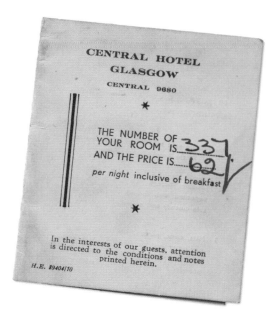

The story of how they started off their married life like millionaires gave them many a laugh over the forty-nine years they were together before George died. Such is the memory of that night in the Central Hotel that Nan has never parted with the receipt and she often thinks of all the famous stars of the 1950s who slept under the same roof as she and George did on the day they started off their long life together.

♣ On September 7, 1978 a society wedding took place in Glasgow. Over 200 guests attended the wedding of Cynthia, daughter of Marcus Stone, a sheriff in the city at the time, and Kenneth Lyon, whose family owned a department store specialising in fine stationery. Eminent guests at the wedding included the late John Smith MP, who went on to become Labour Party leader, the Scottish singer, Kenneth McKellar, and Ian Bankier, now chairman of Celtic FC, who was best friends with Cynthia's brother, Donny. The band keeping everyone's feet tapping that night was the Doug Wyllie Combo.

Cynthia and Ken lived close to one another in Lenzie on the outskirts of the city and had originally booked the Campsie Glen Hotel for their reception but as the number of guests on the invitation list grew, they realised that the dance floor there was not going to be big enough. The decision was taken to change the venue to the Central Hotel which Cynthia's parents knew well.

Above: Celebrity guests at the wedding included John Smith MP (top) and Kenneth McKellar.

Cynthia, who was only nineteen to Ken's thirty-one, recalls it was a very windy day and she looked like a 'tornado' in her long white crepe dress with lace insets in the sleeves. The dress was bought by her mum at an auctioneer's for £12 but at the other end of the scale, Cynthia's veil, which was made out of pure silk attached to a skull cap, was bought from Daly's department store in Sauchiehall Street and emptied the wedding purse of £50. That was only a fraction of the total cost of the society affair which came to £3,500 – a staggering amount for those times!

The marriage lasted thirteen years and, in 2007, Cynthia married her present husband, Peter, in an occasion which could not have been more different from her first wedding. This time the happy couple celebrated in style with a flamenco wedding and Cynthia danced down the aisle to Bizet's Carmen!

Above: Cynthia in her bridal dress.

Above: Anne and Andrew on their wedding day 1963.

Below: Richard Muir and his partner Cara Franchi.

When Ann Muir's son, Richard, and his partner, Cara, took her and his dad, Andrew, into the refurbished Grand Central Hotel in June 2011 they were treated to champagne and canapés courtesy of the management. However, the hospitality wasn't just for Ann and Andrew's praise for the job Principal Hayley has done on the renovation of the grand old building. The couple received their VIP treatment due to the fact that on July 10, 1963 they had held their wedding reception at the Central Hotel after taking their marriage vows in Burnside Parish Church. Along with 120 guests, the newly-weds had enjoyed baked Alaska and danced the evening away to the sounds of Louis Freeman's Band, a regular act in the city's Green's Playhouse ballroom as well as in the Central Hotel.

Andrew has particular reason to be thankful that all the scaffolding had been taken down when he visited the refurbished Grand Central. Back on that night in 1963, his best man and a few of the other guests decided to give him a bit of a send-off before the couple set off for their honeymoon on the island of Sark. Work was being carried out at the time on the outside of the building and the new groom was swiftly relieved of his shoes and socks and sent out to walk on the scaffolding in his bare feet. Fortunately Andrew completed his feat without incident, though one can only imagine the hand-wringing and head-shaking the current Health and Safety Executive would go through if such a prank took place on scaffolding planks these days.

In 1988 Ann and Andrew returned to the hotel to celebrate their silver wedding anniversary, but Andrew's memories of the Central Hotel go back even further than his 1963 wedding reception. Three years earlier he had been walking past the entrance to the hotel when a crowd of young men came out. The smiles on their faces said it all because staying at the Central Hotel was the Real Madrid football team who had lifted the 1960 European Cup the previous evening. The Spanish team had beaten Germany's Eintracht Frankfurt 7–3 at Hampden Park in front of 135,000 people in a game still regarded as one of the greatest ever played.

Above: Match programme for the European Cup Final, Hampden Park, 1960.

❧ Tom Love is a man used to public speaking so the idea of making the father-of-the-bride speech when his daughter, Sharon, got married to Allan Mackin on June 30, 2007 did not bother him one bit. The couple had chosen the Central Hotel (then called the Quality Hotel) for their reception after the marriage ceremony in the St Francis of Assisi Church in Baillieston.

Neither of them had ever been in the Central Hotel before they came to book their wedding reception but the magnificent staircase swayed their decision – they loved it at first sight! It was the perfect setting for having photographs taken and allowing the bride to have a Scarlett O'Hara in *Gone With The Wind* moment as she descended the stairs in her rose-coloured, widely hooped, long-trained gown. They were also happy with the large function suite which had lots of room for dancing.

All went well until the meal was coming to an end. Sharon noticed the staff were taking a long time to serve dessert and when she saw her cousin going for some wine because there was no one serving it she made a mental note to complain. Tom had also noticed something was not right – every member of staff had left the function suite and had been away for several minutes. Then the staff returned, lining up around the room, and the MC had taken Tom aside, whispering in his ear.

He explained there was a 'situation'. There had been a terrorist attack at Glasgow Airport and now there was a report of a bomb in Central Station and the hotel had been put on standby to evacuate. Just what the father-of-the-bride wanted to hear! The staff had been called from the room to be briefed and, if the need for evacuation went ahead, the bridal party and guests, in all their wedding finery, had to take their lead from them.

'If I say the word, just follow me,' the MC said to a now very nervous Tom.

Thankfully, the worst did not happen and everyone had an enjoyable and unforgettable celebration of the couple's union. While her father remained on tenterhooks, Sharon and Allan danced the night away, oblivious until the next morning of how their wedding reception could have been seriously disrupted.

Before the wedding, Tom had visited the hotel on several occasions over the years and he knew its interior was losing some of the grandeur it once had. When Sharon suggested it as a venue for the wedding reception he allowed the hotel's good points to override any misgivings he may have had. By 2007 the hotel, he said, was becoming like a 'Dishevelled Duchess' – still grand but frayed around the edges!

Bottom: Sharon and Allan pose for pictures on the hotel's magnificent staircase.

Left: the Grand Room set out for their guests.

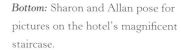

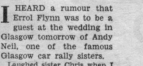

🔔 Andy Neil – her real name was Annie but as she had always been a tomboy she adopted the male soundalike – could control the steering wheel of a rally car beautifully but controlling the rumour of a film star attending her wedding was a different matter.

It was September, 1956 and one of the famous rally-driving Neil sisters was getting married in St Margaret's Church in Tollcross, Glasgow with the reception afterwards in the Central Hotel. A rumour went round the city that Errol Flynn was to be a guest at the occasion (even though Andy was not much of a follower herself) which caused more than a stir amongst fans of the swashbuckling Australian-born actor.

Right: Andy ready to walk down the aisle with her father, George.

Below: How the *Evening News* reported the pre-wedding girls' night out; and (left) the elusive Mr Errol Flynn.

Andy was marrying another rally-driving ace, Francis Dundas from Dumfries, whom she had met, not surprisingly, at a rally. Andy and her younger sister, Chrissie, well and truly made their mark in the rallying world, winning a number of accolades. Highlights

Police patrol for Andy's wedding

I HEARD a rumour that Errol Flynn was to be a guest at the wedding in Glasgow tomorrow of Andy Neil, one of the famous Glasgow car rally sisters.

Laughed sister Chris when I telephoned the Neil home at Tollcross today: "I heard that one, too. There's nothing to it. I think there's a few wild yarns being circulated."

It looks as though it's going to be anything but a quiet wedding. Three hundred guests will attend the reception in the Central Hotel tomorrow evening.

The police are putting on a special "parking patrol" to fit the anticipated 150 cars into adjoining side streets.

Distance outdone

Andy is marrying Dumfries rally star Francis Dundas in St. Margaret's Church, Braidfauld Street. They met, naturally enough, at a rally.

After the wedding she'll go to live in Dumfries.

But the sisters will still be driving together. Their next big date is the Monte Carlo in January.

"And," says Chris philosophically, "Dumfries isn't really so far away. Francis has the road taped. His best time for the journey to Glasgow is 66 minutes."

Which isn't bad for a 75 miles stretch!

Andy Neil is toasted by her sister Chris and friends at a pre-wedding "hen party" in Glasgow last night.

include successfully completing the Monte Carlo Rally not just once, but twice, in 1954 and 1955, with Andy at the wheel and Chrissie navigating. In 1958, when Andy was expecting her daughter, Candy, Chrissie navigated the Monte Carlo for a third time with her brother-in-law at the wheel.

The sisters' father, George, was one of the largest pig farmers in the Glasgow area and Andy learned her driving skills at the wheel of pig trucks. She happily donned dungarees and wellies to help out on the farm but was well known for putting on the glamour for nights out in Glasgow in places like the Rogano restaurant in Exchange Place and the 101 restaurant in Hope Street, both close to the Central Hotel.

Even without the presence of Errol Flynn, the wedding was a society highlight. Three hundred guests were invited and police were called in to put on a special 'parking patrol' to fit an anticipated 150 cars into streets adjoining the Central. The event was covered by the media and some guests briefly left the reception to go out and buy the early edition of the next day's newspapers in order to read all about it!

Andy passed away in 2004 at the age of 80 so memorabilia of those times in the 1950s are all the more precious to her family.

Above: The sisters in rallying action in Hastings.

Left: A wedding guest went to get the early editions of the next day's papers, to see how the press had reported the still-ongoing wedding.

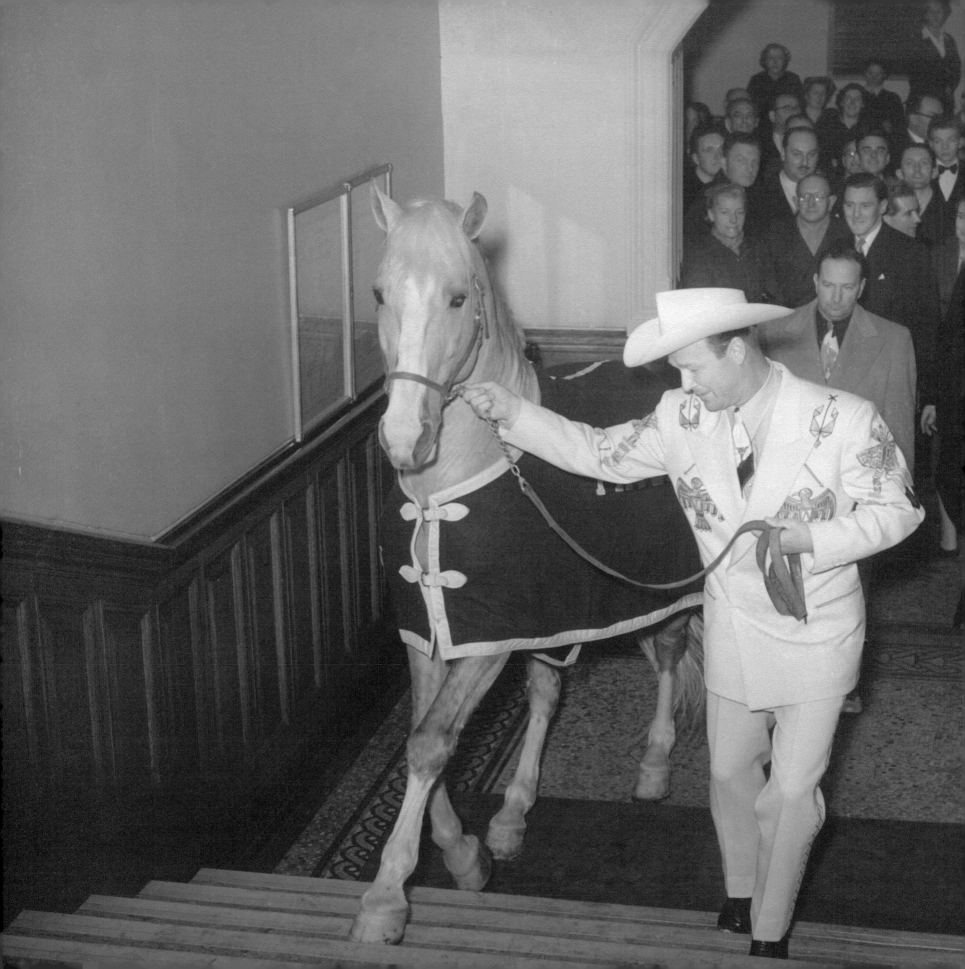

Hollywood on Hope Street

I f there was ever a corner worth standing on for a photographer hoping to get a snap of a celebrity in Glasgow then the corner of Gordon Street and Hope Street outside the Central Hotel was it. For almost four decades – from the 1940s through to the 1970s – everyone who was anyone in the celebrity world came to Glasgow to perform in the many theatres the city had to offer including some long-gone like the Empire, the Metropole, the Alhambra and St Andrews Halls (which went up in flames in 1962) and some that still exist today like the King's, the Pavilion and the Citizens. Most of these celebrities visited or stayed in the Central Hotel and they came to

With a throng of amused onlookers at his back, Roy Rogers leads Trigger up the main staircase at Central Hotel.

Above: Princess Margaret in 1978.

perform serious drama and/or comedy, to sing and/or dance – anything which would entertain the people of the city. It was said if you could entertain a Glasgow audience you could entertain any audience in the world.

As well as the stars sprinkled with showbiz glamour there were other well-known faces from the world of sport, politics and royalty who visited or stayed in the Central Hotel. The late Princess Margaret is known to have stayed in the hotel, Prince Philip has dined there on more than one occasion and when the Queen came to Glasgow to mark the start of her Silver Jubilee tour on May 17, 1977 unprecedented numbers turned out to see the procession which had been organised from a suite within the Central Hotel. The Queen and Prince Philip had travelled to Glasgow on the Royal Train on which they were staying during their tour of the country but they came down past the hotel's back entrance to join up with the rest of the procession heading to Glasgow Cathedral for a Thanksgiving Service.

As you turn the following pages, you will come face to face with some of the many well-known people who have crossed the Central's threshold.

Right: Jimmy Durante at the Central Hotel, 1956. Known as 'Schnozzle' because of his large nose, Durante (1893–1980) was an American entertainer. Singer, piano-player, comedian and actor, Durante was a well-loved, popular personality from the 1920s till the 1970s.

Opposite: Nat King Cole in Glasgow, April 1954. His unforgettable dulcet baritone voice gave him international stardom as a solo star, but he started first as a jazz pianist and rose to fame through the big bands and jazz band sound. He was one of the first black American musicians to host his own TV shows. He was also known for being a collector of pipes!

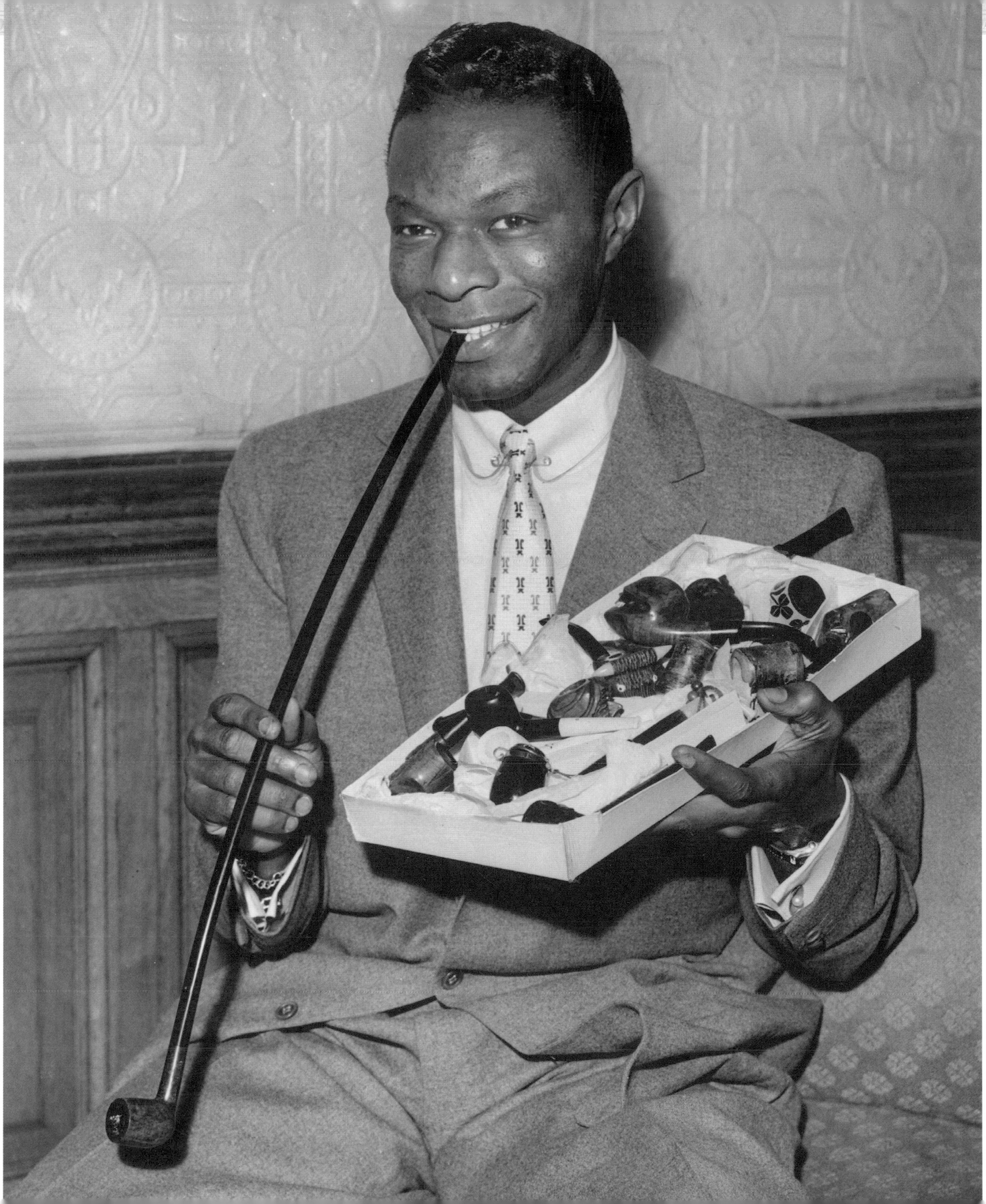

Other famous faces seen at the Central over the years include (clockwise from top): silent movie icon, Charlie Chaplin, with Harry Lauder; comedy duo, Abbott and Costello, seen here in a shot publicising *Buck Privates Come Home* (1947); legendary crooners, Frank Sinatra and Bing Crosby; and dancer, Fred Astaire.

Main picture: Danny Kaye, on arriving at Central Station, tries out one of the piper's bagpipes, June 1949.

Inset: Empire Theatre's programme featuring *The Danny Kaye Show*. The Glasgow Empire was a variety theatre in Sauchiehall Street. It opened in 1897 and was infamous for its tough audience. Many stars performed there, including Laurel and Hardy, Sir Harry Lauder and Andy Stewart. Danny Kaye was a favourite. It closed in 1963 and an office block now stands on its site.

Main image: Guy Mitchell waves to crowds of admirers from the window of the Empire Theatre. Born Al Cernick, the son of immigrants from Yugoslavia, Mitchell (1927–1999) was an American big band and traditional pop singer and international recording star. He came to the fore with Columbia Records with a string of hits that was to span the entire 1950s. Mitchell went on to host his own variety show on ABC Television in the USA and starred in movies and TV Specials.

Sammy Davis Junior, born in Harlem, New York, performed in the Glasgow Odeon on May 15, 1963. The singer, dancer and all-round entertainer stated in an interview with the *Evening Times* that although his career earned him a lot of money it was at the expense of seeing nothing other than the inside of hotel rooms and theatres.

Opposite page: Jean Simmons, the London born actress, seen here relaxing in a comfy seat at the Central Hotel in March 1949, visited Glasgow on several occasions and received an honorary degree in the city. She also attended charity balls held in the City Chambers.

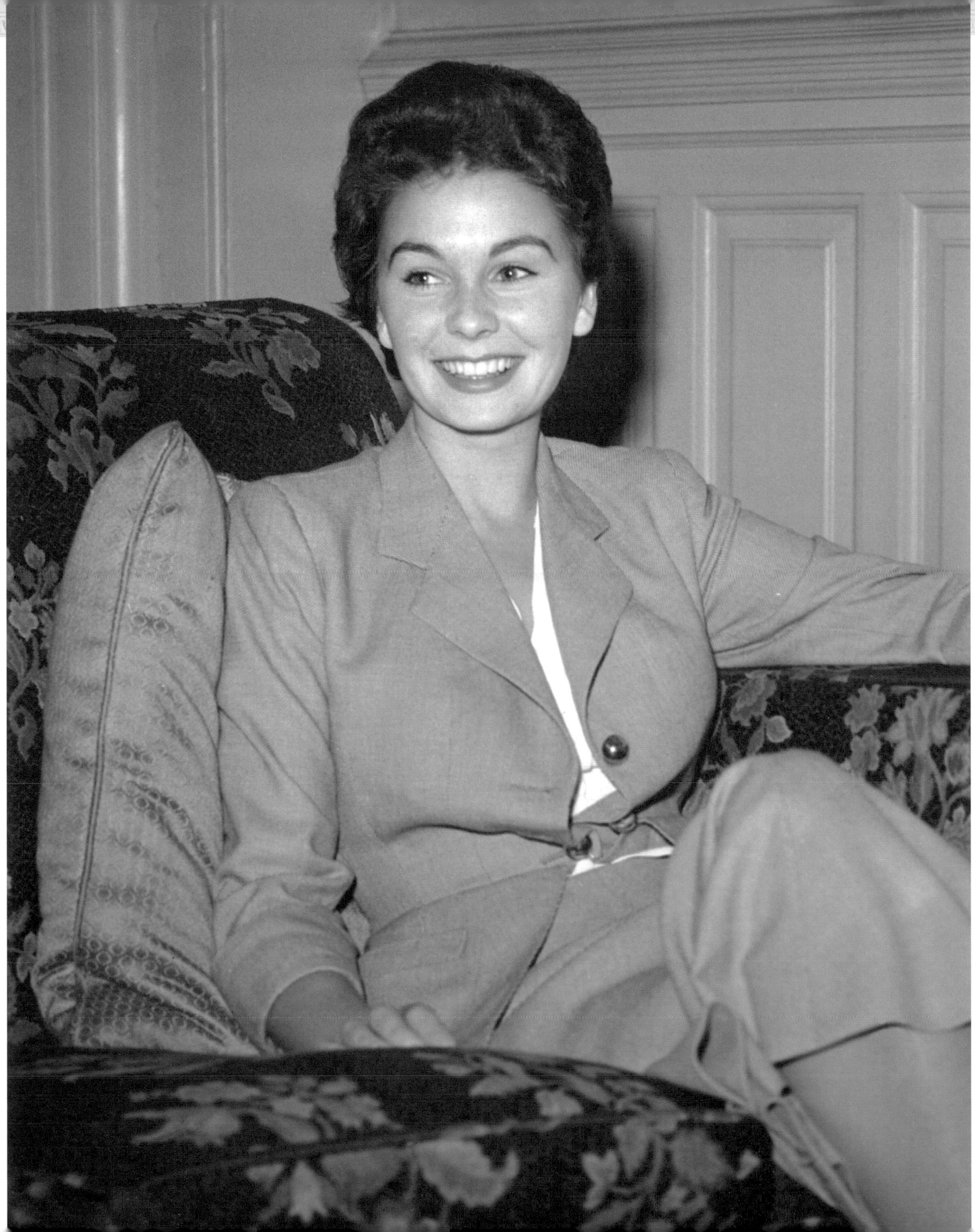

Memories of a Page Boy

Desmond Lynn was just fifteen years old and 4ft 10in high during the mid-1950s when he reckoned a Central Hotel page boy job was for him.

When it came to tipping, whether you were a page boy, chambermaid or head chef, Roy Rogers ensured no one missed out because the film star drew up a list of who should receive his gratitude with amounts given according to staff status.

Desmond had reason to smile when Roy Rogers and Trigger rode into town. Desmond galloped out of the Central Hotel to spend the £5 tip the cowboy and his trusty steed handed over for helping to carry some of the many suits the star had brought for his stay in Glasgow.

Stardom could have beckoned for Desmond, but sadly when Paul Douglas, star of *The Maggie,* a 1954 comedy about a puffer partly filmed in and around the Central Hotel, asked the hotel for a page boy to take a small part in the film, it was Desmond's day off.

After his stint as a page boy, Desmond became a porter and when Abbott and Costello visited thousands of fans screamed for the comedy duo. So did Desmond, but not because he was a fan. As Lou Costello leaned out of a window over the Central Station concourse and waved to fans, he pretended he was about to fall out. What fans couldn't see was Bud Abbott holding his pal's belt to keep him in place, but Desmond is convinced the belt was close to breaking.

Below: Former page boy Desmond Lynn has fond memories of his old colleague, Central Hotel doorman Jimmy Cawley, who would give him a nod when someone rich or famous was due, which meant he could hang around to take their suitcases to their rooms thus ensuring he got the big tips.

Unusual requests weren't unusual in the Central Hotel showbiz world and when American crooner Billy Daniels visited he asked Desmond to take him to a record shop – to buy his own records. Daniels wanted to perfect his performance in front of the bathroom mirror, but it was Sunday and the only place open was the famous Glasgow Barras. Billy got his record, but not before having to sign hundreds of autographs for fans who'd spotted him. As for Desmond, he got a large tip.

When it came to that other great comedy duo, Laurel and Hardy, who took time to wave to thousands of fans in Hope Street from the hotel staircase window, gentle (or perhaps not so gentle) persuasion had to be administered when it came to tipping. Desmond had accompanied them to the third floor and although staff members were instructed never to take photographs or ask for autographs he broke the rule. When he offered Oliver Hardy his pencil, the comedian commented on how small it was. 'Not as small as your sixpenny tip,' replied Desmond, at which point the duo laughed and handed over a princely five shillings each.

American TV star Broderick Crawford, Richard Green, star of TV's *Robin Hood* series, Lady Churchill and singer Frankie Laine – who insisted on frying his own steak on a mini grill in his room – are just a few of the names that trip off Desmond's tongue. He also met Jock Stein, then captain of Celtic FC, in what is now Champagne Central.

Desmond reckons his most lucrative job was cleaning shoes –

Above: Celtic's Jock Stein, 1954.

situated in the first floor Gents toilet, the tips were great. However, Desmond once had to point out to Scottish stage and screen star, Charlie Sim, when he cleaned his shoes, what the tin at his feet was actually for.

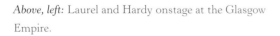

Above, left: Laurel and Hardy onstage at the Glasgow Empire.

Above, right: Laurel and Hardy with sponsor Alf Ellsworth (centre) at the Glasgow Empire, June 1947.

Right (both pictures): A ten-minute walk from Central Hotel along Argyle Street takes one to the Britannia Panopticon Music Hall, Trongate, where a young Stan Laurel first took to the stage in 1906.

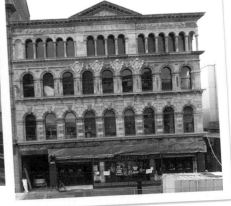

Roy Rogers and Trigger

Above: Trigger smiles obligingly for the camera.

After flying into Prestwick Airport to begin a UK tour, Hollywood cowboy Roy Rogers and his famous Palomino horse Trigger signed the register at the Central Hotel in February 1954 then took a walk up the wide staircase much to the amazement of other guests and staff. In a great promotional stunt, it was reported that Trigger had his own suite in the hotel when, in fact, he was housed in stables nearby. Trigger was presented during his stay in Glasgow with a giant kilt which fitted right over his hindquarters from behind Roy's saddle.

What excitement there was in the home of children Margaret and Wilma McBean when their aunt, Hannah Allan, arrived not only to tell them the story of Trigger's famous walk up the hotel stairs but also to give them a present of a copy of the picture (see page 82) proving it. The girls were aged eight and twelve and to them, like most children of the time, Roy Rogers was a hero. They loved watching his TV show, *The Roy Rogers Show*, which ran from 1951–57, and had seen many of his films.

Hannah, from Newhouse, worked in the Central from the age of seventeen until she left in 1956 and at the time of Roy Rogers' visit she was Head Telephonist. At work she was always addressed as Miss Allan. Rebecca Allan, Hannah's sister and mother of Margaret and Wilma, had also worked in the hotel reception or on the switchboard until she got married in 1936.

Accompanied by his wife Dale Evans (who was known as Queen of the West to his King of the Cowboys), Roy arrived at the hotel with trunk-loads of embellished suits, white Stetson hats and hand-tooled boots in preparation for the many stage appearances he was to make during his lengthy UK tour. After Glasgow the couple headed east to appear at the Empire in Edinburgh and whilst in the capital they visited an orphanage where they met one of the residents, thirteen-year-old Marion Fleming. This encounter changed the dimensions of their family life, for they were so taken with the youngster that they invited her to spend the summer with them and eventually she became their ward, adopting the name Mimi.

Roy Rogers and Trigger became a team in 1938 and in the following decades they appeared in 80 films and 101 episodes of their TV series and made countless public appearances. Roy was so distraught when Trigger died in 1965 at the grand old age of 33 that the news was not made public for over a year and up until 1989 he was still signing autographs 'Roy Rogers and Trigger'.

Roy Rogers and Trigger sign in at the Central Hotel, 1954.

Opposite: November 1947 and Mae West enjoys a joke with ex-boxer Kid Lewis at the Central Hotel. She was in Glasgow appearing in *Diamond Lil* at the Alhambra while she stayed at the Central Hotel. Designed by the architect Sir John James Burnet, the Alhambra Theatre opened in 1910 at the corner of Waterloo Street and Wellington Street. Elegant and seen as a leading theatre ahead of its time, it was famous for glamour, humour, variety, pantomime, ballet and opera as well as dance. The theatre was demolished in 1971.

Right: Opera singer Gigli with pianist Dino Fedri. Gigli was singing at the St Andrews Halls in March 1955.

Below: Staying at Central Hotel, Howard Keel, veteran of Hollywood musicals, and, in 1984 starring in TV's *Dallas*, was appearing at the Theatre Royal where backstage he was introduced to Glasgow's new Lord Provost Bob Gray.

Family Connections

In the early 1940s Britain was entrenched in war and sirens instilled fear into every citizen as families scattered from their homes to take refuge in air-raid shelters. However, in many ways life went on as 'normal' and in 1943 Elizabeth Lauder Hamilton, great niece of Scottish international entertainer Sir Harry Lauder, left school to become a student. Glasgow's Stow College had just started a hotel management course whose aim was to train and prepare students for jobs in some of Scotland's and the world's finest hotels. Gleneagles, the George Hotel in Edinburgh and Glasgow's Central Hotel would benefit from the experience new graduates gained and to ensure training was authentic students spent time working in a hotel.

Betty, as she's known, was sent to the Central Hotel to complement her classroom work and for a period of one month at a time she trained on reception, worked in the kitchens and finally became a chambermaid. In those days there were few en-suite bathrooms. Instead, should a guest have to spend a penny during the night a chamber pot was provided. Naturally, they had to be emptied by the chambermaid though fortunately Betty had an ally when it came to this chore. During her stint around the bedrooms, she was placed into the safe hands of an experienced chambermaid. 'I can tell you've never had to empty a chamber pot before, so I'll do that,' her tutor told her, much to Betty's relief.

Above: Sir Harry Lauder pictured in 1939; and the bill from one of his Empire Theatre appearances.

Right: Ralph Richardson (top), and Laurence Olivier.

A chambermaid had to clean twenty-eight rooms during her daily routine which included making up the beds with pristine linen sheets, complete with blankets and bedspreads. No duvets in those days. Wages were meagre and the only way to make more money was to keep in the good books of the guests, who could tip generously – or not as was sometimes the case.

The faces of many guests, famous or otherwise, are a blur to Betty, who reminisces about the dozens of people she saw hanging around in the mornings dressed in bathrobes, queuing to get into the bathrooms. However, during her stint on reception a couple of celebrities did cross her path. One morning she raised her head to see a well-built man about 6 ft tall standing in front of her. It was English actor, Sir Ralph Richardson, knighted in 1947, who would go on to star as Alexander 'Sasha' Gromeko alongside Omar Sharif in

the 1965 box office smash *Dr Zhivago*. Sir Ralph was there to pay his bill and he was immediately followed by another revered English star of stage and screen who, according to Betty, had a voice as soft as velvet with exceptional tonal quality. Unfortunately, she didn't recognise him and had to ask his name in order to provide his bill. 'Laurence Olivier,' was his softly-spoken reply.

If she wasn't providing the stars with their bills or emptying chamber pots, Betty was sweating over a hot stove – literally, for the temperature in the kitchens could be sky high. Betty recalls a fellow student fainting but there was no time for tea and sympathy and the kitchen staff simply walked over her until she came round and was well enough to take up her post again. Ultimately, the heat in the kitchen proved too much for Betty and a hotel career was not to be, but she's never forgotten her time behind the doors of 99 Gordon Street's Central Hotel.

Betty's story would not be complete without some further reference to her great uncle, Sir Harry Lauder. Born on August 4, 1870 in Portobello, his first professional engagement in Larkhall came about after encouragement from his fellow mineworkers who had been able to enjoy Harry's singing as they toiled deep underground. In 1905 Sir Harry wrote and sang 'I Love A Lassie' for a pantomime in Glasgow's Theatre Royal. The song made him a British phenomenon and by 1911 international stardom and 1,000-dollars-a-night tours of the United States beckoned. One of Sir Harry's greatest admirers was the American singer and dancer, Danny Kaye, and it was as one of the world's greatest performing artists that Danny visited Glasgow in 1949 to perform at the Empire Theatre (and stay in the Central Hotel).

In 1912 Harry was top of the bill at Britain's first-ever Royal Command Performance in front of King George V and during a Royal visit in September 1917 some five years after that King George V was barely a whisker away from the Central Hotel. He had stopped at Central Station to review 222 men and women from the Merchant Navy who'd been torpedoed by enemy submarines. Wearing a naval uniform and accompanied by officials of

the Caledonian Railway Company, King George presented medals to the seafarers and spoke with four stewardesses who had survived the sinking of the Lusitania.

Above: Danny Kaye clowns around with the pipe band before watching Celtic defeat Rangers 3–2 in the Glasgow Charity Cup final, May 6, 1950 in front of 81,000 fans. The game became known afterwards as 'The Danny Kaye Final'.

Cary Grant went up in the world at the Central Hotel

YOU'LL never guess who I had in my lift today, mum!

Hollywood star Cary Grant was going up in the world when he stepped into the elevator at Glasgow's Central Hotel in 1961.

It wasn't the Bristol-born star's first visit to the city. Back in the days when he was still called Archie Leach, he performed as a dancing stilt-walker at the Britannia Panopticon Music Hall in Argyle Street. Although we doubt he went back to visit!

In reality, the presence of a star passenger probably failed to faze the lift boy. After all, the hotel was used to welcoming some of the biggest names in showbiz.

Left: A 1961 visit to Central Hotel from Hollywood royalty in the form of Cary Grant, as reported in the *Evening Times*.

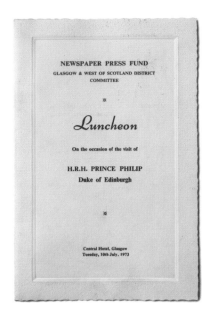

NEWSPAPER PRESS FUND
GLASGOW & WEST OF SCOTLAND DISTRICT
COMMITTEE

Luncheon

On the occasion of the visit of

H.R.H. PRINCE PHILIP
Duke of Edinburgh

Central Hotel, Glasgow
Tuesday, 10th July, 1973

Right: Prince Philip enjoys a laugh at a newspaper press fund lunch in the Central in July 1973. Standing behind him on his right is Peter Fort who was Banqueting Services Manager. Peter worked at the Central between 1969 and 1983 and took over the position previously held by Raymond Pagani for thirty-six years.

Right: Billy Connolly made an appearance at the hotel during the 1980s.

This page: Gene Kelly came to Glasgow in April 1953 with his producer, Arthur Freed. They were looking for a location in which to film *Brigadoon*. Although Gene Kelly was keen to film the story, about an enchanted eighteenth-century Scottish village which only appears for a day once every 100 years, in the country where it was based, it never happened. MGM decided it would be too costly and instead the 1954 musical, which also starred Van Johnson and Cyd Charisse, was filmed in the US on a studio set.

Hearts of Hope

This picture of British-born comedian and entertainer Bob Hope (1903–2003) was taken on January 26, 1956 when he was guest of honour at the Roosevelt Memorial (Polio) Fund annual dinner-dance held in the Central Hotel. Three hundred guests paid two guineas a ticket to attend the star-studded event which was also attended by civic leaders including the then Lord Provost of Glasgow, Andrew Hood.

Bob and a number of other high-profile celebrities, including Douglas Fairbanks Jnr who was the star attraction in 1955, attended several of these annual fundraising functions over the years. The hotel staff loved it when Bob was a hotel guest for he was as much of an entertainer off stage as he was on and was legendary for his impromptu singing, dancing and joke-telling sessions.

The Roosevelt Memorial (Polio) Fund was a joint Scots-American venture set up in Glasgow in 1951 to raise money for the aftercare of polio victims. In 1954 it was estimated some 16,000 children north of the border had used equipment financed by the fund in school clinics. The bank balance then stood at £2,286, £1,000 of which had been set aside to be used if polio reached epidemic proportions. Thankfully, this never happened.

After suffering a paralytic illness (believed at the time to be polio but more recently attributed by others to Guillain-Barré syndrome) at the age of

39, American President Franklin D Roosevelt was never able to walk unaided again. He spent the rest of his life seeking new ways to improve not only his own life, but the lives of others afflicted by polio.

The very first Birthday Ball, held in communities all over America, took place in 1934 on January 30 (Roosevelt's birthday) and raised over a million dollars. The American Birthday Balls ended in 1945 with Roosevelt's death but the fund-raising work continued through a charity called the March of Dimes. In 1954 a massive field trial of a vaccine created by a Jonas Salk, a young physician whose research was financially backed by the March of Dimes, was carried out. Its success saw Salk's vaccine licensed for use on April 12, 1955 and by the 1960s the disease was eradicated throughout most of the world.

Sadly many were left with the legacy of polio and fund-raising efforts for their care continued. On December 3, 1970 a Scottish Golf Ball was held in the Central Hotel to raise money for the Roosevelt Memorial (Polio) Fund. Tickets cost £3 10s and the event was attended by prominent golfers of the day including Eric Brown, Bernard Gallacher, Ronnie Shade and Dave Thomas.

Above: Bob Hope presented cameras to children Jennie Milton of Forres and Eric Cuthbertson of Paisley, who immediately used them to take pictures of the star to show to family and friends.

Left and opposite: Accompanying Bob on stage was British singer and actress, Yana, who reached the height of her fame in the 1950s and 60s. She appeared regularly on *Sunday Night At The London Palladium.*

Below: Franklin D Roosevelt, United States President (1933–45), photographed in 1933.

Celebrity Mania

When the Central Hotel opened its doors in 1883 it quickly became apparent there was something staff would have to get used to – celebrity-chasing crowds. From those early days after US boxing champion, John L Sullivan, crossed its threshold, fans of the stars have bribed, conned and cajoled their way into catching a glimpse of their heroes and heroines in the hotel and its surroundings.

Nowadays celebrity publicity is generated in many ways, but in pre-internet and digital days publicity was captured by making 'a big entrance' and the celebrities loved it when crowds turned up to greet them. For example, back in September 1952, Danny Kaye got off his train in Central Station, grabbed an attending pipe major's mace and proceeded to march through thousands of screaming fans and into the hotel. Not for him, sneaking in through a side door or tunnel entrance – at least not until his next visit when he was persuaded in the name of his own safety and that of his fans to inform no one of his imminent arrival.

Another celebrity who experienced a frightening display of celebrity mania was Dorothy Lamour. In May 1950 she was trapped in her car outside the Empire Theatre by a baying mob intent on getting a glimpse of their Hollywood siren before she headed off to the Central Hotel for the night. The words fear, terror and horror must surely have been in her thoughts as hoards of fans crawled all over her limousine.

On another occasion, the arrival of husband and wife stars, Larry Parks and Betty Garrett, at the Empire Theatre on June 19, 1950 caused such a riot that crowds of their fans risked life and limb as they surged between two passing trams.

PROGRAMME
Continued

7. THE JOHN TILLER GIRLS - *Dance Time Again*

8. THE KENWAYS - *Thrills in the Air*

9. FRED LOVELLE - *Watch his Lips*

10.

DOROTHY LAMOUR

with
SAM MINEO
AT THE PIANO

The Management reserves the right to refuse admission to the Theatre, and to change, vary or omit, without previous notice, any item of the programme

A decade later it was the turn of the Beatles. On October 5, 1963 the Fab Four took up residence in the Central Hotel during a three-night mini-tour of Scotland. They had been booked in months earlier under their own names and were performing in the city's Concert Hall (demolished in 1968) in Argyle Street. Although fans in their thousands turned up outside the Central to welcome the group, six lucky girls did manage to get over the threshold and meet their heroes – Joyce McFarlane (20), Rosetta McFadyen (17), Jean Gifford (18), Christine Steele (16), Janet Thomas (16) and Myra Millar (17) were pictured with the Fab Four in the Central after winning a 'Meet The Beatles' competition in the *Daily Record*.

Later that night, thinking they were safe after being smuggled out of a side door of the Concert Hall, the Beatles' five-minute journey back to their hotel ended with them

Left: The Fab Four on a visit to Dundee.

Below: The *Daily Record* reports on the Beatles' visit in 1963, and shows them in the Central with the six lucky competition winners.

Opposite page, top: Dorothy Lamour's appearance at the Glasgow Empire.

Opposite page, bottom: Danny Kaye escorted by police amid throngs of fans on the streets of Glasgow.

fighting off thousands of screaming fans in Hope Street and Gordon Street – and not for the last time.

On April 30, 1964 a return visit by the group to Glasgow, where they were appearing in the Odeon Cinema in Renfield Street, resulted in 300 fainting cases, a 'Beatles Fans In Riot Night' newspaper headline and a hose being turned on fans during a visit they made to a television studio. The same year on October 21, fans smashed windows, threw objects at mounted police and overturned cars when the Beatles played the Odeon for a second time. On both these occasions, and much to the relief of the Central Hotel, the group chose to stay elsewhere!

Rockin' in the Central

Below: Robert Plant on stage.

By winter 1972, Green's Playhouse in Glasgow had said goodbye to the big bands like those of Joe Loss and Duke Ellington who played the top-floor ballroom while cinema lovers watched the latest screen releases downstairs. The ballroom became a discotheque called Clouds and the 4,000-plus capacity cinema turned into a concert venue for bands like the Rolling Stones, Deep Purple and Led Zeppelin. In September 1973, Green's became the Glasgow Apollo. The Style Council performed in the last show to be held there in June 1985. Any hope of resurrection was doomed following a fire, and the building was torn down in 1987.

However, it was Led Zeppelin and their entourage who were demolished courtesy of the management of the Central Hotel after the first of two night gigs at Green's in December 1972.

On December 3, after that first night gig, Jimmy Page, Robert Plant, John Bonham and John Paul Jones came off stage as thousands of fans spilled into Renfield Street with 'Stairway to Heaven', 'Black Dog' and 'Whole Lotta Love' ringing in their ears.

You would have thought what better way was there for band and crew to relax but in their hotel with a good meal and maybe a TV or two thrown out of the window as was the wont of many rock bands. Wrong! Although the rock and roll show that was Led Zeppelin could do no wrong in the early 1970s they were short of the one thing that the Central Hotel management insisted on – a tie! No tie, no entry to the restaurant and that left Led Zeppelin feeling 'Dazed and Confused' just like the song from their 1969 debut album. An argument ensued, but it was to no avail. The hotel management would not budge – or lend ties – as reported in the following morning's *Daily Record* and Led Zeppelin decamped to another hotel. What a 'Heartbreaker' the manager of the Central must have been back then!

Beryl Beattie was just sixteen when she won a beauty and talent competition, organised by Canadian talent scout Carroll Levis, in Glasgow's world-famous Empire Theatre in the 1950s. Beryl, who went on to become a dancer in Glasgow's Alhambra Theatre, won the competition after her mum Thora spotted an article about it in *The Sunday Post* newspaper – an article which helped to attract over 300 entrants from across Scotland. Carroll, who hosted the Carroll Levis Discovery Show, interviewed each contestant on stage before the audience were asked to applaud the girl they wished to win. The talent scout was looking for a young lass to represent Scotland with the title 'Miss Annie Laurie' after the famous Scottish song.

To this day, Beryl puts her success down to the dress she wore that night. It was a midnight-blue evening dress bought by her mother, but under the stage lights the colour looked more like royal blue. Beryl's main rival that night wore a green dress and she reckons she won the competition because the audience was mainly made up of Glasgow Rangers supporters.

Her prize was a two-week audition trip to New York where she met, among others, singer Eddie Fisher and actor Robert Alda, father of Alan who starred as Hawkeye Pierce in the smash television series *M*A*S*H*. She also had dinner in the Big Apple with Tommy and Jimmy Dorsey of Dorsey Brothers fame (Frank Sinatra was among the stars who sang with them in their heyday).

Beryl's two-week, all-expenses-paid trip to New York wasn't her only prize that evening. The night of the competition she was taken to Glasgow's Central Hotel for dinner where she met a teenage Tommy Steele who'd been performing at the Empire and was staying at the hotel. Minding her manners among such prestigious company, Beryl had dinner in the same room as the *Half A Sixpence* star while his fans screamed his name outside in Hope Street. The room they occupied on the first floor is now a

conference suite. As you would expect, the Central Hotel ladies' room was rather opulent and Beryl can still recall the mirrors surrounded by light bulbs, just as they would be in any fine backstage dressing room.

Tommy wasn't the only star Beryl bumped into in the Central Hotel. Sitting nearby at dinner that evening was singer Frankie Laine and on a later visit Ella Fitzgerald smiled at her in a corridor. She also got an impromptu invitation to join another star for dinner. On this occasion, she was walking along a corridor in the hotel when she was passed by heart-throb American singer Vic Damone. As they met he dropped his room key, which Beryl hurriedly bent down to pick up. However, he also bent down and their heads clashed with an almighty thud. Apologising profusely, the singer invited Beryl to join him for dinner that evening, an offer she politely turned down because 'well-brought up girls just didn't do that' in those days.

In the decades that have passed, whenever she has walked past the Central Hotel, and more lately the Grand Central Hotel, Beryl's heart misses a beat as she recalls those heady days. She has paid a visit to the refurbished hotel and is delighted with the results of everyone's efforts to bring it back to its former glory but she does wonder if Vic Damone can still recall that clash of heads so long ago in the Central Hotel corridor.

Top: Beryl Beattie with the Dorsey Brothers (right) along with a female chaperone and a Roosevelt Hotel representative.

Above: Ella Fitzgerald.

Below: Vic Damone.

The Autograph Hunters

Above: Charlotte dressed up for a night out in 1950.

Top left: Maime Nolan and her friend Bridie Gallagher were on breakfast duty in the Central's dining room when they managed to get Fred Astaire and Bing Crosby to put their autographs on the back of a luncheon menu.

Top right: Jimmy with his autograph book.

For a teenager fascinated by the world of stage and screen, Jimmy Friel could not have wished for more than to have an aunt who was in charge of the cocktail bar in the Central Hotel during some of the best years of Glasgow's theatre industry.

Celebrity guests, returning to the hotel following a evening entertaining audiences, were often happy to sit at the bar and chat quietly with Charlotte Kilday – who came from the same area in Glasgow as the Townhead Terrors – as she went about her work and they enjoyed a relaxing, late-night drink.

Charlotte worked in the hotel for over two decades between the 1940s and 1960s and, says Jimmy, became a bit of a 'confidante' to the stars, especially those who made return visits to the city. She particularly enjoyed the company of Lena Horne, the velvet-voiced singer, actress and life-long civil rights activist who broke new ground for black performers in Hollywood.

Fred Astaire and Cyd Charisse, all expressed thanks to Charlotte for her tactful manner with a signed photograph. The young Jimmy, who had been theatre-mad ever since a first visit to the Metropole Theatre on a family outing to see the Logan family, was over the moon when presented with a photograph signed to him from Lena Horne.

Knowing his love of stage and screen, the autograph book that Charlotte's eldest sister, Susan, had given him as a birthday present, when he reached his teenage years in 1954, was often behind the bar in the Central when she knew celebrities were on the guest list. It became an ever-growing treasure trove of autographs from the likes of Frankie Laine, Roy Rogers (and Trigger), Dale Evans, Gracie Fields, Guy Mitchell, Bob Hope and Nat King Cole.

Jimmy was the envy of his school pals – and in particular for one set of signatures in his autograph book which had nothing to do with the theatre. On December 8, 1954 Scotland was beaten 4–2 by Hungary at Hampden in a friendly match before a crowd of 113,000. The Hungarian Golden Team was legendary in the 1950s, dominating records in football globally.

'Charlotte got on well with Mae West too,' says Jimmy. 'She said she was the kind of person Glasgow people would like. Charlotte was always very discreet in her private conversations though and would never reveal intimate details.'

The stars showed their appreciation with personally-signed photographs. Dean Martin, Jerry Lewis and Jack Buchanan, the Helensburgh-born entertainer who became a big name on the musical comedy stage and whose film career included *The Band Wagon* with

Above: The female staff swooned when Hollywood idol Jack Buchanan came to stay. The Helensburgh-born actor was known for his good looks, elegance and debonair manner which went with his immaculate dress sense. He starred in more than thirty films and enjoyed the lifestyle success brought including a Rolls Royce which he had specially made for him. In December 2011 the 1933 Phantom II sold at auction for £54,300. Buchanan died in London in 1957 at the age of 66.

Above left: Lena Horne (1917–2010), American singer and actress.

Far left: Martin and Lewis, the comic duo formed by Dean Martin and Jerry Lewis, who made their debut together in 1946.

Left: Frankie Laine unexpectedly met on the concourse of Glasgow Central Station by soldiers of a Scottish regiment.

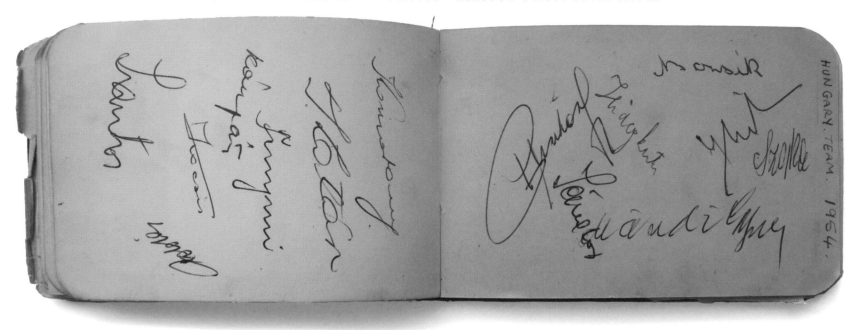

Above: Jimmy's autograph book showing the signing of the Hungarian football team including Ferenc Puskas.

Above: Jimmy and Ella, the girl who was to become his wife, on their first date which took place in the Central Hotel.

Barring the 1954 World Cup, from June 4, 1950 the team recorded 42 victories, 7 draws and only one defeat when they lost 3–1 to Turkey on February 19, 1956.

The result at Hampden on that cold December day in 1954 was the closest any team had come to beating the Hungarians in a friendly competition since 1950. Earlier in the year, on May 23, 1954 Hungary had seen a humiliated England off the pitch after a score of 7–1 in a game played at the Ferenc Puskas Stadium in Budapest. The stadium was named after Ferenc Puskas, Hungary's greatest football player ever and regarded as the top goal-scorer of the twentieth century. He was in the team which played against Scotland at Hampden. The jubilant winners were staying in the Central Hotel and Charlotte managed to get young Jimmy an early Christmas present with autographs from all of the players, including Puskas! It was some tale to tell his pals – thanks to his aunt he had the autographs of the most famous football team in the world!

Autographs aside, Charlotte and the Central Hotel have had more than a passing influence on Jimmy's life. In 1958, when he was seventeen,

Charlotte set him up on a date with a girl who was looking for a partner for her all-expenses-paid staff dance. She, too, was only seventeen and she worked in Hill's, the bookies. The dance was in the Central. It was the first grown-up formal affair in a grand hotel for both of them, and the fact they did not have to pay anything for their first date made it all the better. Jimmy, in his new dark suit and Brylcreemed hair, must have impressed for some years later he and Ella Pisacane were married.

Charlotte and her two sisters worked all their lives in the hotel trade. Her sister, Nelly, also worked as a waitress at the Central and was serving dinner at the dance on the night Jimmy and Ella met for the first time! Charlotte was the youngest and, despite the sometimes antisocial hours of her job, she loved it.

'She never married, was full of fun and enjoyed life to the full. She was a very independent woman and always very well groomed,' says Jimmy.

🐾 Iain Henderson has collected autographs for over forty years and at the peak of his collecting period the Glaswegian had almost 10,000 of them. Among his Bob Hope, Bing Crosby and Diana Dors signatures, an autograph he managed to get at the Central Hotel still sticks in his mind to this day.

In July 1979 former Manchester United and Irish superstar footballer, George Best, signed for Hibernian. It was a troubled time for the Edinburgh club who were heading for relegation and so-called bad boy Best was hired on a 'pay per play basis'. He failed to save Hibs from relegation that season, but the number of fans through the turnstiles increased dramatically thanks to his appearances.

Best was on a trip west in the summer of 1979 to Glasgow's Central Hotel when Iain got lucky. He just happened to be passing by when he spotted a rather superior-looking coach parked outside the hotel. Inquisitive as ever, he asked who was around and a short time later George Best appeared from the door of the coach. As luck would have it, Iain happened to have a football programme with him that contained a picture of George and the superstar duly signed it for him. Courteous and easy to talk to is how Iain describes the footballer, who then went into the hotel to attend a dinner and presentation.

Left: George Best runs out for his debut game for Hibernian, against St Mirren in 1979.

Although he still has around 500 autographs left in his collection, Iain sold the George Best signature, but he has never forgotten that late afternoon in the summer of 1979 when a footballing giant signed his football programme.

🐾 It seems it took more than a tickling stick to bring a bit of happiness to Liverpool comedian Ken Dodd during his stay in the Central Hotel in October 1972. After a plate of fish and chips in the Malmaison for Doddy and a friend, according to observers, the Diddy Man from Knotty Ash was not tickled pink when presented with his bill of £12.50.

However, after Restaurant Manager Joe Moretti explained that fourteen members of his staff had been held back for an extra hour in order to serve the two diners, it seems the situation was resolved. Of course, as you would expect, the bill wasn't for any old fish supper served up in a wrapping that carried the previous day's news and sport and Doddy's fish was complemented with strawberries and cream, some fine wine and lager.

Above: The *Daily Record* gave a lunch in the Central on December 22, 1976 in honour of Scotland's Best Young Swimmer of 1976, David Wilkie. He'd triumphed at the Olympics held in Montreal that year winning both gold and silver medals.

Inset: Ken Dodd.

Below: The evergreen Cliff Richard, and Central Hotel stationery bearing his autograph.

The Townhead Terrors

Like any establishment where stars of stage and screen gather, the Central Hotel received its fair share of autograph hunters. However, during the late 1940s and early 1950s two teenage girls in particular stand out: thirteen-year-old Jean Smith and her fourteen-year-old friend Mary Devine, both from Townhead.

Jean and Mary were in their element hanging around outside the hotel or in the foyer in order to get signatures from the likes of Chico Marx, Bing Crosby, Frank Sinatra and Danny Kaye. Sometimes catching a star-studded signature was merely a phone call away, for having kept tabs on who was in town, one of the girls would simply call the hotel reception and ask if a star was in their room. Quite often, without any questions being asked, their call was put through and after arranging an autograph appointment with the star, it was simply a case of turning up at the agreed time. When that didn't work an obliging doorman would sometimes tip them the wink on who was in residence. During their time as successful autograph hunters, Jean and Mary were treated to tea with Margaret O'Brien – one of cinema's most

popular child actresses – and when Larry Parks and his wife, Betty Garrett, stayed in the hotel, they invited the girls to their show at Glasgow's Empire Theatre and even sent a taxi to take them there.

In 1949 *The Sunday Post* newspaper had carried an article dubbing the girls the 'Townhead Terrors' and when the same paper ran an article on Principal Hayley's refurbishment of the Central Hotel in 2010 an amazing set of coincidences unfolded.

Jean Smith (now Jean McMillan) hadn't seen the article, but three days after it appeared she was in Glasgow. When she got on her bus to go home Jean spotted a woman looking at her. She recognised the woman, but couldn't place her so asked who she was. Her name was Margaret Lyons and although she hadn't seen Jean since their childhood she had recognised her. Jean was astonished when Margaret told her that she had seen her picture, as a thirteen-year-old, in an article in *The Sunday Post* a few days beforehand.

Above: American actress and singer Pearl Bailey's autograph.

Below: Mary Devine's autograph book, displaying the signature of film star John Boles, along with a *Sunday Post* cutting featuring the girls themselves.

Then *The Sunday Post* was contacted by a man called Michael Carlin and he told them that back in 2004, he and his brother, Mark, had come across an old autograph book their mum had owned. Sadly, she had passed away, but it turned out that their mum was Mary Devine, Jean's autograph-hunting friend. Along with the autograph book there was a photograph of Mary and Jean with Larry Parks and Betty Garrett, taken for an article in the *Weekly News* about the teenage autograph hunters. Jean still has her own copy of the photograph as well as a cutting of the article which her dad had kept and a letter from Metro Goldwyn Mayer confirming that Jean and Mary had been in the company of Hollywood child actress Margaret O'Brien, who'd treated them to tea in the Central Hotel.

Right and below: The girls enjoy a laugh with American stage and film actor Larry Parks and his wife, actress and comedienne, Betty Garrett.

Between 1949 and 1951 the girls themselves became celebrities, having taken part in a BBC radio show to speak on air about how they went about gathering autographs from the many celebrities of the time. The singer Frankie Laine was one of Jean's favourite celebrities. He had top ten hits with 'High Noon' and 'I Believe' and once put on an impromptu performance on the Central Hotel balcony overlooking the Central Station concourse. The place was thronged with fans and when the show was over Frankie used a tunnel system linking the hotel to the station to escape. The balcony has gone, but guests of the refurbished hotel can enjoy the same view as Frankie by looking out over the station concourse from Champagne Central.

The autograph of multi-talented actor, singer and dancer Danny Kaye was also captured by the Townhead Terrors. Famed for his roles in *Hans Christian Andersen* and *The Secret Life of Walter Mitty*, it seems his on-screen happy-go-lucky demeanour didn't always transpose to his real-life persona, for according to Mary's sister, Betty, she recalls Mary coming home after getting his autograph and telling her he 'was a bit of a

Left: Jean McMillan with Michael (left) and Mark Carlin.

moaner'. Nevertheless, he was another celebrity in the autograph book of the Townhead Terrors.

Boxing and the Central Hotel

Above: John L Sullivan.

Right inset: Peter Keenan.

Below: Peter Keenan takes to the ring in relaxed, pre-fight mode, in the Grand Room of Glasgow, Central Hotel.

A history of the Central Hotel wouldn't be complete without the mention of boxing and its association with the hotel – an association that goes back almost to the building's beginnings. In December 1887 just four years after it opened, American World Heavyweight Champion, John L Sullivan, stayed in the Central while in Glasgow as part of his Scottish tour. Sullivan, recognised as the last heavyweight bare knuckle champion and first heavyweight gloved champion, must have liked the Central because in 1910 he spent the honeymoon of his second marriage in the hotel.

Fast forward to October 1937 when the pride of Glasgow, flyweight Benny Lynch, defended his world title at Shawfield Stadium against England's Peter Kane. The *Daily Record* newspaper paid ex-boxer and successful Hollywood film star, Victor McLaglen, to do a ringside report of the fight. McLaglen had won an Academy Award for Best Actor for his role in the 1935 film *The Informer* and later in his career he was to play Squire 'Red' Will Danaher who had an epic screen fist-fight with John Wayne in the 1952 movie *The Quiet Man*. He had also once fought Airdrie's Dan McGoldrick.

McLaglen arrived at Central Station with Welsh heavyweight, Tommy Farr, and both stayed at the Central Hotel during their visit. As their train drew into Central Station, McLaglen was approached by Glasgow newsagent, John Shaughnessey, who had been his military servant in Mesopotamia (now modern Iraq) during the First World War, and the pair had the chance to reminisce for a little while before McLaglen and Farr were whisked away to their hotel.

James J Braddock, another famous World Heavyweight Champion who was immortalised by Russell Crowe in the film *Cinderella Man*, stayed at the Central when he was guest of honour at a professional boxing show staged in the hotel in November 1967. And finally with a name synonymous with boxing in Glasgow, and the first, and so far only, Scottish boxer to win two Lonsdale Championship belts outright at bantamweight, Peter Keenan loved the Central

Hotel and promoted regular professional bouts there throughout the 1960s. As a promoter he brought Sugar Ray Robinson, Sonny Liston and Muhammad Ali to Glasgow (the latter two passing through the Central) and when American World Lightweight Champion Archie Moore came to Paisley for a personal appearance he spent some time in the hotel.

The Grand Central has carried on the boxing tradition established by the Central Hotel and a night of ringside activity was enjoyed by 400 fans in the Grand Room of Glasgow shortly after the hotel's reopening in September 2010.

MORRISON PROMOTIONS
PRESENTS A
CHAMPIONSHIP BOXING EVENING

99 Gordon Street Glasgow G1 3SF

GRAND CENTRAL HOTEL GLASGOW
Friday 29th October 2010
···► £2.00 ◄···

In Cold Blood

It wasn't just the good and the great who stayed in the Central Hotel. Sometimes the bad would bed themselves down in the splendour of the Victorian building and one man inexplicably linked with two of them is Detective Lieutenant John Thomson Trench.

In December 1908, 83 year old spinster Marion Gilchrist was beaten to death at her home at West Princess Street in Glasgow's West End. Despite there being a wealth of jewellery in her home, a brooch was the only item reported stolen. Shortly after the murder a German called Oscar Joseph Slater had set off by sea for New York but earlier that year he had checked into the Central Hotel, signing the register as Mr A Anderson. Posing as a wealthy businessman, he had stayed in the hotel with his mistress and a maid, though both women were probably prostitutes. Slater was a con man known to the police.

Prior to the murder, a caller to Marion Gilchrist's house had been looking for someone called Anderson and Slater had been seen trying to sell a pawn ticket for a brooch, so he came under suspicion for the murder and was extradited from the United States. He was tried and sentenced to hang, but his sentence was commuted to life imprisonment after a petition.

John Thomson Trench, who had worked on the case, had always had serious doubts about Slater's guilt and in 1914 he took his misgivings to the Secretary of State for Scotland. However, despite an inquiry, the conviction was considered safe. Trench then found himself kicked out of the police force for communicating information to a third party without the permission of his chief constable.

Trench's encounter with Slater wasn't the only link he had with the Central Hotel. In 1912 he was asked to help in the apprehension of a man

called Karl Graves. Graves, who had checked into the Central, was part of a German intelligence network and, with war waiting in the wings, he had been tasked with gathering information about Rosyth dockyard. Posing as a medical student, he had also been poking around the premises of Glasgow engineering company, William Beardmore. However, the newly formed MI5 was onto Graves and when two of its agents came to Glasgow to nail him they requested that Trench work with them. Graves, known as the 'Glasgow Spy', was nabbed in the Central Hotel and became the first person to be arrested under the Official Secrets Act (1911). He was given a prison sentence of 18 months.

In 1919 Trench died, aged just fifty, and although there were many attempts to clear his name of wrongdoing in the Oscar Slater case the record wasn't set straight until 1999. The Slater case has often been cited as one of Scotland's biggest miscarriages of justice. Because of his tenacity in bringing the case to the attention of the authorities, a plaque was unveiled in Trench's memory at Glasgow police headquarters in Pitt Street after a lengthy campaign by John Scott from Cambuslang and a *Glasgow Herald* journalist. Although Trench wasn't completely exonerated, he'd had an otherwise unblemished record with Glasgow Police and the ceremony paid tribute to the fact he acted in good faith.

As for Slater, he was released from jail in 1928 and went on to live out his life in Ayr while Graves, despite going on to work for the British Secret Service, ended up with blackmail and grand theft charges against him in the United States.

Above: Oscar Slater.

Below, left: A letter written in German by Graves, under the pseudonym James Stafford Esq., which came into the possession of Burroughs Wellcome & Co (as the putative sender) after being returned to sender by the Glasgow General Post Office.

Below: An artist's impression of Karl Graves.

History Flickers into Life

Bottom: John Logie Baird conducting an early television experiment on a London roof, 1927

A history of the Central Hotel would be incomplete without paying tribute to its historical link with John Logie Baird, the man credited with the invention of television.

Born in Helensburgh on August 14, 1888, Baird took an electrical engineering course at Glasgow and West of Scotland Technical College, now the University of Strathclyde. After graduation he went to Glasgow University to upgrade his diploma to a Bachelor of Science. The university noted his perfect attendance and the fact he played a full part in campus life, but due to the outbreak of the First World War he did not complete his degree. Instead, he tried to enlist in the Army but an illness when he was two years old had left him with weak lungs and poor circulation and this rendered him unfit for service.

Early in 1923, and in poor health, Baird moved to Hastings on the south coast of England where he rented a workshop. Using an old hat box, scissors, darning needles, bicycle light lenses, a tea chest and glue, he demonstrated it was possible to transmit moving images. In March 1925 after a move to London, he was able to demonstrate moving silhouette images to the public in Selfridges department store and in October the same year transmitted the first television picture – the head of a ventriloquist's dummy. His short-distance demonstrations of sending live TV pictures down a phone line began to receive worldwide attention.

A public television company called Television Limited was formed in London in 1926 with Baird as its managing director. The company was based in Motograph House in the heart of London's theatre district. In May 1927, a transmitting device was set up in Motograph House while in a semi-darkened bedroom on the fourth floor of the Central Hotel in Glasgow a receiver had been installed. Baird was in London with the transmitting device while 438 miles away in Glasgow was old friend and fellow enthusiast, Captain O G Hutchinson, with the receiver. A demonstration in front of selected people, including Professor Taylor Jones of the Chair of Natural Philosophy in the University of Glasgow took place on Tuesday, May 24. It was a grainy, black and white image which flickered into life. The following evening another transmission was sent and a third on Thursday, May 26. After each subsequent transmission improvement in quality was noted and John Logie Baird's features, right down to his mass of wavy hair were recognisable on a two-inch screen.

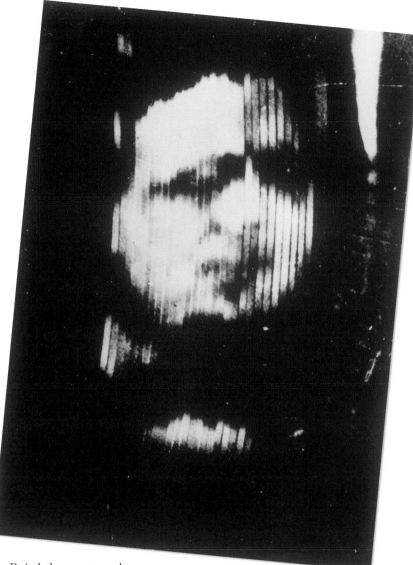

TELEVISION MARVELS

Glasgow Looks In On London

YOUNG SCOTTISH INVENTOR'S GREAT ACHIEVEMENT

The young Glasgow engineer, Mr John L. Baird, who came into prominence eighteen months ago as the inventor of television—a process by which it is possible to reproduce, either by wireless or over telephone wires, whatever is placed before the receiving end of the instrument—has made an epoch-making step in the development of electrical communication by successful demonstrations of the use of the apparatus in telephonic communication between Glasgow and London.

The first demonstration was given on Tuesday night, when transmission took place between Motograph House, London, and the Central Station Hotel, Glasgow. The experiment was repeated with equal success on Wednesday evening and again last night. Expert opinion is that the chief difficulties with which the brilliant young inventor was faced have been overcome, and that important and far-reaching developments in television by radio may be looked for in the near future.

DEMONSTRATION IN GLASGOW

SUCCESSFUL EXPERIMENTS

For many months Mr Baird and his partner, Captain O. G. Hutchinson, have been quietly at work perfecting the apparatus by which the actual images of people can be sent through the ether. The success obtained over short distances encouraged the inventor to undertake the bold experiment of establishing televisory communication between the first and second cities of the Empire. No doubt sentimental considerations also influenced Mr Baird in choosing his native city as the setting of the greatest test to which his invention has yet been put. In a semi-darkened room on the fourth floor of the Central Hotel the receiving televisor was installed under the superintendence of Captain Hutchinson, and the transmitting end in London was in charge of Mr Baird himself.

PROFESSOR'S IMPRESSIONS.

Among those who were privileged to be present at the first demonstration was Professor E. Taylor Jones of the Chair of Natural Philosophy in the University of Glasgow, who, in an interview with a representative of "The Glasgow Herald" in his study at the University yesterday gave his impressions of the process by which Glasgow obtained its first look into London. "I saw it all quite distinctly," said Professor Taylor Jones, speaking of the screen transmission. The Professor explained that the transmission took place over a trunk telephone line, and owing to induction effects in the line the images were unsteady at times, but at other periods they were remarkably steady and clear. The first object to be shown at the transmitting end was from still life—the head of a dummy. It was an office boy who had the distinction of being the first to exhibit himself to the eager gaze of those who were watching the receiving screen in Glasgow. The operator at this end spoke instructions through the telephone which were immediately obeyed by the image on the screen. At request the boy turned his head from side to side, put his hand to his head, and even protruded his tongue—and each action was plainly seen at the receiving end.

A REMARKABLE ACHIEVEMENT.

Recognising the great difficulties of light and shade which had to be contended with, Professor Taylor Jones expressed surprise at the clearness with which the image came through. The parts of the head have to be transmitted in very rapid succession, but so swiftly did the apparatus work that the impression given was that the face was being presented not piecemeal but as one whole. Herein was the key to the success

ordinary listening-in set can work the televisor. The progress made by the inventor in scientific research has served to reduce greatly the compass of the apparatus. The receiving televisor now in use is contained in a cabinet approximately 32in. in length by 28in. in height.

Mr Baird's object is to link up television with wireless broadcasting over any distance, and definite steps towards this end are now being taken so that in the near future it may be possible for a person on this side not only to establish telephonic communication with America but to see the person to whom he is speaking. We are informed that a number of receiving televisors are now in process of completion, and that they will be distributed to different centres within the next few weeks in order to test reception by radio, which obviously should give better results than the use of the land line, which is subject to so many outside disturbances. The advance of scientific research in electrical communication is so swift in these days that it is difficult for the man in the street to keep pace with its developments; but Scotland has reason for satisfaction that one of her sons is keeping well in the forefront, and bids fair to realise his immediate ambition, which is to have television receiving sets on the market at a comparatively moderate cost before the end of the year.

FUTURE DEVELOPMENTS.

It would be idle to forecast the developments that may be expected in television in the sphere of world communication. But it is interesting to note Mr Baird's prophecy, speaking at a recent meeting in London, when he remarked that within ten years people would be able by means of the televisor to see such topical events as the finish of the Derby or the Boat Race. Questioned regarding future possibilities, an authority on the subject said the picture presented at present by the televisor was admittedly a small one, but in his view the greatest difficulties had been overcome. The enlarging of the picture should not present any serious obstacle; it was merely a question of light at the receiving end.

WHAT TELEVISION IS.

The process by which Mr Baird has arrived at his discoveries are best described in his own words. In the course of an interview with a "Glasgow Herald" representative quite recently he said that a great deal of confusion existed in the minds of the public between television and the sending of photographs and pictures by wireless. Television was not the sending of photographs by wireless, but was the instantaneous transmission of living and moving scenes. In the television process whatever was set before the transmitting apparatus was reproduced simultaneously, with every detail of movement, in the image on the screen of the receiving apparatus. The ambition to achieve a form of television had been the cause of experiments for the past 50 years, said Mr Baird. His own, and the latest contribution towards the accomplishment of what was formerly a scientific abstraction, began in practical form four years ago with

Baird then set up the Baird Television Development Company Ltd and the first transatlantic TV transmission between London and New York came in 1928. The inventor also became the first person to demonstrate colour TV.

His successes did not go unnoticed at the Central Hotel. Its main function room (now the Grand Room of Glasgow) was named after the man whose 'brain was his notebook', a reference to the fact he rarely wrote anything down. When the new Grand Central Hotel opened after its refurbishment in September 2010 there was never any doubt Baird would remain as much a part

Above: The first recorded television picture.

Right: How the *Glasgow Herald* reported the story in May 1927.

Opposite, bottom: John Logie Baird conducting an early television experiment on a London roof, 1927.

of its fabric as the sandstone and mortar that constructed the Victorian building. A suite is now named in his honour and a plaque, first unveiled in 1988 by his son Malcolm and his assistant Ben Clapp, takes pride of place in the main reception area. Many have wondered why John Logie Baird chose the Central Hotel back in 1927, but the answer is straightforward. Apart from being the leading city hotel, the receiving equipment used would have been transported from London by train so it was a simple matter to move it from the adjoining Central Station.

How ironic then that one of the first calls the maintenance team received after the 2010 reopening was from a guest who couldn't get their flat-screen TV to work – in the John Logie Baird Suite. This was quickly fixed by putting new batteries in the remote control – how times had changed! The inventor died on June 14, 1946 at the age of just fifty-seven but his legacy lives on through the coveted John Logie Baird Awards for Innovation and it is fitting that the 2011 awards ceremony took place on March 11, 2011 in the Grand Central Hotel.

Below: A May 2010 *Daily Record* article on John Logie Baird's son Malcolm and his memories of his father. It was published prior to the hotel's refurbishment when the memorial plaque to Baird was re-sited to the lobby, and a suite was named after the inventor.

Victoria Lee was diagnosed with Crohn's Disease in 1995. She has gone through over fifty operations and endured multiple organ failure. While bedridden for almost a year, Victoria had dreamed of returning to Barbados with her husband, Robin. The couple had married there and she wanted more than anything to wear her swimming costume once again on the Caribbean island. When it seemed her dream might come true, she was deeply upset at not being able to find a costume that would hide the fact she wore a colostomy bag and she decided to design swimwear not only for herself, but for the other 150,000 men, women and children in the UK who have to wear a colostomy bag.

She went to work and after sketching designs and sourcing materials that didn't cling to the body, Victoria came up with a unique belt which could be clipped inside the swimwear to hold a stoma bag in place and hide the fact that it was being worn. She paid a visit to an organisation who know best about invention and innovation – the John Logie Baird Awards Programme – and after they gave Victoria advice on how to secure a patent, she set up Glitter Beach, her own company, which produces beachwear and other clothing suitable for stoma and non-stoma patients. (Part of the company profits go towards further research into Crohn's Disease.)

Scotland has the highest incidence of Crohn's Disease in the world and, with a global figure of 8.2 million stoma patients, Victoria has found a way of making a real difference to many people's lives. It was this which led to her being awarded the 2011 John Logie Baird Social Enterprise Innovator Award in front of 300 people at a ceremony in the Grand Central's Grand Room on March 11, 2011.

Right: Victoria Lee is stunned as she is announced a winner at the John logie Baird Awards in Grand Central Hotel.

All Tuned Up

No 'grand' hotel would be complete without a grand piano and as guests take their first steps up the Grand Central Hotel staircase, which once felt the footsteps of Roy Rogers and Trigger, they can't miss the black baby grand on their left-hand side.

One man who tinkled the ivories on many an occasion in the Central Hotel was Terry Martin. Born and brought up on Glasgow's south side, Terry, whose mother was a cinema pianist, had been playing the piano since primary school. On his return from serving with the RAF in Hong Kong during the 1950s, he began playing in prestigious hotels such as the Central, Gleneagles and Turnberry and whether entertaining with Dixieland, turning out renditions from the Great American Songbook or playing classical pieces, his performances were always accomplished.

Terry was happy to take requests from his audience. Songs by Nat King Cole, Ella Fitzgerald and Frank Sinatra – all stars associated with the Central Hotel in days gone by – were always great favourites but he was equally at home playing 'As Time Goes By' or the theme from the Paul Newman and Robert Redford film *The Sting*. According to many, Terry had the left hand of American jazz pianist Erroll Garner and the right hand of seven-times Canadian Grammy Award winner Oscar Peterson. He was also responsible for putting together many of the bands of the day who played at prestigious railway hotels such as Glasgow's Central Hotel.

Sadly, the Glasgow man who performed in front of Princess Anne and the Duke of York during his career never got to sit down at the piano in the refurbished Grand Central Hotel. Often referred to as 'Mr Happy' due to his smiling persona, Terry Martin was entertaining just five days before he sadly passed away on January 14, 2011.

Above: Sir Douglas Bader was a famous Royal Airforce fighter pilot, who lost both legs in an accident in a RAF training run in 1931, but went on to win honours for his role in the Battle of Britain and the Second World War. His life was chronicled in a book and film called *Reach for the Sky*. He was later knighted for his work for the disabled.

Above, left: Terry Martin.

Below: Elizabeth Joyce in her prime as a resident singer in the Central Hotel.

A singer since childhood and a former fashion model, Elizabeth Joyce was an entertainer who appeared regularly in the Central Hotel. From the mid-1960s for twelve years, when it came to wedding receptions, bar mitzvahs and grand balls, she wooed audiences with her renditions of everything from jazz to the classics.

Many famous people would drop into the Grand Room to hear her perform, but one particular night she had to be forgiven for not recognising one of them. The occasion was a Royal Air Force dance in the Central Hotel's Grand Room and Elizabeth was asked to sing a romantic number for none other than Sir Douglas Bader, the Second World War ace flyer credited with over two dozen aerial victories during the war.

Resident singer most weekends during her stint in the hotel, Elizabeth went on to tour with Scottish singer Alasdair Gillies.

Central's Celebrity Appearances

Many famous names have walked through its doors, but the Central Hotel has made a few celebrity appearances of its own:

Above: A screenshot from *The Maggie* showing the hotel entrance and a rain-soaked Gordon Street.

Top, right: DJ George Bowie introduces The View on stage, and (below) Champagne Central during Clyde 1's *Live On Location*.

In 1954, the hotel appeared in the Ealing Film Studios' comedy, *The Maggie*, made by Alexander Mackendrick. The laughs start when the captain of a dilapidated old Clyde 'puffer' boat called *The Maggie* tricks an American businessman into letting him carry his valuable cargo. Several scenes were filmed on Islay and in Glasgow. The film reflects life as it was in the 1950s when Glasgow was an industrial city with a thriving riverside (and not short of few characters among its citizens!).

Champagne Central set the scene in March 2011 for Clyde 1's *Live on Location*. For five mornings in a row, DJs George Bowie and Suzie Maguire presented the breakfast show from the Grand Central and the Central Station's concourse. Acts they interviewed live included Emma's Imagination, The View, Parade, Wonderland, Shayne Ward, the former X-factor winner, and Scottish singer-songwriter, Carrie Mac. With crowds gathering every day, the event was a great success.

Between 1996 and 2004, the Celtic Connections Festival Club would take place at the Central, featuring the cream of the acts from the festival playing after-hours shows and impromptu jamming sessions well into the small hours of the morning.

Dior by Dior, the autobiography of fashion supremo Christian Dior, famous for his 'New Look' collection of 1947, was first published in 1957.

Top, left: Dior's autobiography, and the catwalk at Gleneagles Hotel during the Dior fashion show of 1955.
Above: The Gospel Truth Choir's *Live From Grand Central* album.

In it he talks about a visit to Scotland in April 1955 when he was invited by Lord Inverclyde, chairman of the Friends of France (an organisation founded in Glasgow during the Second World War to assist the French sailors from Brest evacuated to the city), and Mr Étienne J Vacher, its honorary secretary, to 'bring over my mannequins' for a soirée they were giving to help raise funds. Étienne Vacher was on the British Transport Hotels' hotel management team and two shows were put on, one at the Central Hotel, and the other at Gleneagles.

You would not normally associate gospel music with Scotland but the Gospel Truth Choir recorded their second album *Live From Grand Central* in the Grand Room of Glasgow in the Grand Central Hotel and then held a concert there to mark its launch in November 2011. The choir was formed in 2007 by a group of friends after they sang at BAFTA-winner Paul Leonard-Morgan's wedding at Luss. There is now a pool of about forty vocalists and musicians who perform for charity and professionally. The choir has performed with Sir Tom Jones. Their first CD was called *Deep Fried Gospel*.

'All in a day's work' – that is what Assistant Front of House Manager, Sandy Fraser, discovered one day on his shift in reception. Since its re-opening, the elegance of the Grand Central Hotel's interior has brought many a request to use the hotel as a venue for fashion photoshoots for magazines. On this occasion it was for the autumn 2011 edition of *The Best Scottish Weddings* magazine. The male model to accompany the bride in her gorgeous gowns had not turned up, but the styling and photographic team were ready for action, so Sandy got roped in, the stylists took over, and here he is making his debut as a model!

Below: Sandy Fraser models for *The Best Scottish Weddings* magazine.

Central Hotel Staff

If housework is something you would rather ignore then spare a thought for the thirty-strong housekeeping team at the Grand Central Hotel. Every day they have to make sure that bed linen and towels are changed, rooms and bathrooms tidied, toiletries like shower gel and shampoo replaced and that all the public areas are pleasing to the eye – not forgetting keeping the chefs in pristine whites!

Head Housekeeper Lynne Doyle is one of only two staff – the other is James Murphy the Executive Head Chef – for whom the hotel

Staff enjoy a Christmas lunch in the kitchens, 1957.

WARNING AGAINST FIRE

Small fires which might have had serious consequences have recently been caused in Staff Quarters through carelessness on the part of the staff.

Do not hang clothes near open or electric and gas fires.

Switch off all electric appliances such as electric irons and heaters, wireless sets, etc., before leaving the room.

Do not throw lighted cigarette ends or matches into waste paper baskets, or leave them lying in any position likely to cause a fire.

Fire is a danger to life and property. Do everything to avoid it.

An old fire safety notice from the staff quarters of Central Hotel.

Protocol Over the Years

🌿 If there was a fire drill, the hotel kitchen staff met on the concourse of Central Station. Jackets and aprons had to be changed before leaving in order to keep up appearances while standing outside.

🌿 Caviar was locked up in a small cupboard in a walk-in fridge. The sous-chef on duty had the key and would issue the caviar as needed.

🌿 Staff were told to always keep on good terms with the housekeeper. She was the most-feared person in the building.

🌿 Older people, so staff were told, always demand more precision and care than younger people: 'Age makes some people believe the world is against them and we have to convince them this is not so.'

🌿 How to address guests was important: if the Queen was a guest she was 'Your Majesty' accompanied by a bow or curtsey at the first encounter. Thereafter, 'Ma'am' was acceptable. Ordinary guests had to be referred to as 'Sir' or 'Madam'.

🌿 At one function in the 1970s, £1,000 worth of cigars were sold.

🌿 Nothing came out of the kitchen on a plate. Everything was always served at the table.

holds long-standing memories. Lynne started in hotel housekeeping in the Central Hotel when she was eighteen before moving on to a larger hotel group at twenty-one. However, she could not resist the temptation to come back to the refurbished Grand Central Hotel despite memories of an awful uniform and polishing kits, and being terrified not only of working in the dimly lit basement where all the laundry was stored but also of scaling the heights to each floor in a noisy lift.

Today, six of the housekeeping team are male, something which would have been unheard of when Lynne started two decades ago. Work starts at 7 am with the cleaning of the front door then throughout the day twenty-seven vacuum cleaners spring into action, with an extra large machine for the Grand Room.

The wide staircase is one of the most talked-about features of the hotel and it always has to look good. Keeping it sparkling clean is another task for Lynne and her team. As well as the brass stair rods being polished till they shine like gold, also on the 'to do' list are polishing the banisters and cleaning the intricately designed railings. Removing accumulated dust from the curls and swirls pattern

of the black wrought-iron railings is done every two months. A multi-purpose cleaner is sprayed onto the railings which are then gently polished with a small round brush. It doesn't take just a few hours or even a day or two to clean the staircase – working in short spells at a time it can take up to a fortnight to get from top to bottom.

Housekeeping also handles lost property – everything from mobile phones to house keys. An amazing assortment of items have remain unclaimed (including a full suitcase of clothes) and after three months they are given to charity.

Above: Housekeeping staff member, Georgina Docherty, keeping the stair ironwork spick and span.

Top, left: Lynne Doyle, Executive Head Housekeeper.

Bottom, left: Just a section of the chart in the hotel's laundry room detailing every room in Grand Central, and the status of its housekeeping.

Mum's the Word

Anna Bain has raised five children of her own but her mothering duties did not stop there. Instead they have included the hundreds of chefs working in the Central Hotel's kitchens over four decades. To them she has always been affectionately known as 'Maw Bain' and the hugs and kisses were in abundance when she met up with her 'boys', many of whom she had not seen for over thirty years, at the chefs' Reunion Dinner held in the hotel in October 2011.

Memories shared that night included one of Anna's first tasks when she was taken on in the kitchen in 1973 – making fruit salad from scratch for a function to celebrate New Year with 1,000 people expected! The bananas were always put in last and there was a huge sigh of relief from Anna when the last slice was in the juice.

Then there was her work in the potato house where all the vegetables were prepared. Potatoes were put in a rumbler – a tubular kitchen appliance with a sandpaper-like inside – to be peeled and the timing had to be perfect. If left on, the rumbler kept on peeling, and peeling, and the potatoes inside could end up the size of peas!

Anna's title of 'Maw' was well earned. She looked after the head chefs in many different ways, including making sure their jackets were immaculate and their breakfast on the table. Heading the small army of chefs then were Jacques Labat who left in 1977 and Stewart Cameron who went to Turnberry in 1982. Jacques Labat was very particular about his cotton chef's hat. It had to have eighteen pleats and be several inches taller than everyone else's. 'Maw' also listened to the woes and grumbles of the chefs down the ranks and, when they went on a night out, glasses with Alka-Seltzer in them were for the next morning's hangovers!

Like the rest of the kitchen staff Anna wasn't allowed up the stairs. The first time she ever went higher than the basement kitchen was to be a buffet maid in the restaurant on the entresol floor. Working in the kitchen could be stressful at times but there were lighter moments with lots of banter and mischief, like the time Anna walked into the larder to discover a skilfully created large butter bust of Jacques Labat.

Few could match Anna's commitment to the Central Hotel. She only hung up her apron for the last time when she retired, at the age of seventy-seven, just weeks before the hotel closed down in 2009.

Above: Anna celebrates her seventieth birthday in 2001 with flowers from manager, Scott Taylor.

Left: This was the scene when a recruitment day was held in June 2010 for the new positions going in the refurbished hotel. Vacancies ranged from housekeepers and bar workers to receptionists and chefs. Management expected a good response but were astonished when 2,000 hopefuls queued for hours to apply for the 150 jobs available.

Chefs' Reunion, October 30, 2011

A Return to Grand Central
"The Legends Live On"

Degustateurs de La Grande Carte

Le Pâté Maison 10/- Le ris de Veau Braisé Empereur 20/-
Champignons sur Croute 5/-

Le Fillet de Sole Véronique 10/- Bisque de Homard 5/-

Les Cailles Sautées 36/- Le Filet Diane 25/-
Les Pommes de Terre Berny 2/- Les Épinards à la Crème 3/-
Chou-fleur Hollandaise 3/-

Crêpes Suzette 4/- Poire Belle Hélène 6/-

Fromages Assortis 3/-

Le Café avec Petit Fours 1/-

Grand Central Hotel
Glasgow

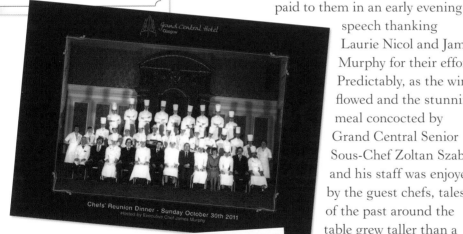

Chefs' Reunion Dinner - Sunday October 30th 2011
Hosted by Executive Chef James Murphy

'My God, we're getting a fight! This is my kind of night!'

Words uttered – in jest – by one of the guests sitting around the table on the evening of October 30, 2011 in the Grand Room of Glasgow in the Grand Central Hotel.

The comment referred to a good-hearted disagreement between a group of chefs, reunited after General Manager Laurie Nicol and Executive Head Chef James Murphy tracked them down from a photograph taken in 1981 in the same room under the Grand Room's fireplace. A few chefs, of course, were missing, but tributes were paid to them in an early evening speech thanking Laurie Nicol and James Murphy for their efforts. Predictably, as the wine flowed and the stunning meal concocted by Grand Central Senior Sous-Chef Zoltan Szabo and his staff was enjoyed by the guest chefs, tales of the past around the table grew taller than a Jacques Labat hat.

It is hard for an outside observer to imagine what goes on behind the scenes in the kitchens of a hotel such as the Central, but the chefs that evening could tell of events that make a Gordon Ramsay workplace look like a temple. For instance, what on earth would Sir Hugh Fraser have thought if he happened to pop his head around the kitchen door to witness a helpless commis being lobbed into the soup kettle because he was a persistent late arrival for work? And you can bet the guys involved in the incident with Wee Shuggie weren't laughing like they were that evening when they were frogmarched to Head Chef's office for getting into a locker room water-bomb fight. Such shenanigans usually ended up in someone getting the sack!

Back in the 'good old days' their hands were black from rubbing their fingers to the bone – using emery paper to clean their stoves – and heaven help them if they were caught using vinegar to clean the inside. Vinegar caused damage which meant Head Chef had to spend money having the stove refurbished and that did not please him at all. Even though the kitchen staff rarely had time to sit down no matter how long their shift, every chef in the room that evening insisted the sense of discipline and dedication instilled during training remained with them.

Throughout the night they reminisced, told tales, remembered long-lost friends and toured the areas which once held the kitchens where they had served their time as chefs. Their sadness at the demise of the hotel prior to Principal Hayley's £20-million investment was discussed, their pride at it being brought back to life as the Grand Central Hotel evident.

Adjourning to Champagne Central to end their evening, the only indication of the passing of three decades was the need for specs to read the menu and – say it quietly – some larger waistlines from enjoying the fruits of their labour over the years.

Top: The menu for the reunion dinner.

Middle: Each guest had a specially-printed placemat featuring the original kitchen brigade group photograph.

Bottom: Zoltan Szabo (left) and James Murphy.

Left: The 1981 kitchen brigade, and all the chefs get together once more thirty years later (below).

Below, left: A sample of the fine dining available to the connoisseurs.

Right: Posing for a final group shot, all the guests who enjoyed the Chefs' Reunion.

From First-Commis to Head Chef

James Murphy's written offers of employment from Central Hotel from 1979 and 1981, showing how inflation affected weekly wages, rising from £48.30 per week in 1979 to £59 in 1981.

'East, west, hame's best' so goes the saying and the chef appointed to put the Central Hotel back on the culinary map is certainly proof of that. James Murphy has cooked his way round the world in the last thirty years and is now back working in the Grand Central Hotel where he once held the position of First Commis Chef.

The Grand Central Hotel Executive Head Chef is putting into practice the skills learned over the years in hotels both at home and abroad and about which he is absolutely passionate. 'If you don't have the passion, forget it,' says James. Top UK hotels he has worked in include the Dorchester, Grosvenor House Hotel and the London Maxim's of Paris. Overseas he has put his culinary skills into action in Germany, South Africa, Hong Kong and Canada.

A graduate of the former Glasgow College of Food Technology, James is probably one of the few people who have actually turned down a much sought-after chef's position in the Central Hotel. In 1979 he was offered the post of First Commis Chef at the hotel at a rate of £43.80 a week. The hotel personnel team were more than a little surprised to get a letter from him saying he was unable to take up the position as he had received a job offer from another hotel – the five-star Dorchester in London. James had decided it was just too good an opportunity to miss and he joined the chefs' brigade there.

Two years later he was chasing a scholarship abroad but the work permit was taking so long to come through that he returned to Glasgow and joined the Central staff as a First Commis Chef under the leadership of Stewart Cameron and at the increased weekly salary of £59. It turned out that coming back to Glasgow at this time was a good move for James for it was when he met his wife, Susan. Prior to walking back through the doors of the Grand Central, James had been Executive Chef at the Hilton in Glasgow for twelve years.

So what has changed over the years? The kitchens for one thing – in the refurbishment they have been moved from the basement to street level where there is much easier access to the Tempus Restaurant and Deli Central. There is also a kitchen on the entresol floor where the Grand Room of Glasgow and other function suites are. Nowadays more work is outsourced and kitchen jobs have become much more efficient, so from a brigade of about forty staff in the kitchen thirty years ago there are now only twelve.

The intricate French food once served in the Malmaison has been replaced with locally produced quality food, simply cooked. However, an exception was made on the night of October 30, 2011 when chefs from the brigade picture taken in 1981 were invited to return to the Central for a reunion dinner with their former colleagues (a brigade picture used to be taken every year with the most senior staff in the front row and the junior staff in the back row).

It was the first time most of them had actually sat down in the role of guest and had such a fine meal served to them. James, and his Senior Sous-Chef, Zoltan Szabo, had prepared a culinary feast for them based on Malmaison menus at pre-decimal prices. It included Champignons sur Croûte at 5s, Le Filet Diane at 25s, Crêpes Suzette at 4s and Fromages Assortis at 3s.

Preparing meals for the Tempus Restaurant and Deli Central is only a small part of the chefs' work at the Grand Central Hotel. On a daily basis the catering demands of the hotel's function areas, from the 500-capacity Grand Room to the twenty-one meeting rooms, need to be met and this can be anything from a finger buffet to a five-course dinner – all in a day's work for James and his team.

A Central Romance

Formality was very much the name of the game when Billy Campbell, now the Executive Head Chef at the Thistle in Glasgow, was offered the opportunity to join British Transport Hotels (BTH) as a trainee chef in 1970 at the Central Hotel. The paperwork for his employment had to be signed not only by Billy, but also by a parent and in the presence of witnesses!

Billy's Kitchen Training Agreement was drawn up on April 7, 1970 and lasted four years until July 31, 1974. In it the guardian who had signed it, in Billy's case his mother, had to agree, along with the trainee, that during the period of training Billy would 'obey the lawful orders of the Employer or his representative' and if he did not, it would

be lawful to cancel his agreement and discharge him. Billy met the terms and four years later on July 31, 1974, after he had risen through the ranks in the kitchen and gone to day release at college, the Kitchen Training Agreement was duly signed providing him with a Certificate of Service.

Billy also had a workplace romance, meeting his wife Marie while learning his culinary skills. As you can well imagine, a hotel the size of the Central, with a large staff to run it, has seen many a romance over the years, but not all of them have had hotel protocol getting in the way of true love. Marie was a cashier in the Malmaison for two years and it took Billy six months to pluck up the courage to ask her out as she was front-of-house staff and he at that time was a Chef de Partie on the roast section.

It was a very upstairs/downstairs scenario, and Billy thought Marie would not want to go out with him but she did. When news of the romance reached the ears of Head Chef Jacques Labat, he called Marie into his office and told her Billy had the makings of a really good chef and he did not need anything to distract him from achieving this, like a woman in his life! Billy had no knowledge of this conversation and it remained that way as Marie only told him about it several years later.

The division between departments even stretched as far as staff functions. About six months after they started going out, each put their name down to attend the 1975 staff dance and Marie was told in no uncertain terms by her head of department that she would not be sitting with Billy at the meal. He had to sit with the chefs, she had to sit with the front-of-house staff – the two departments just did not mix. However, they got together after the meal and had a picture taken. Thirty-seven years later, at the Chefs' Reunion Dinner in October 2011, they stood on the same spot to be captured on camera yet again. And on this occasion, they were able to sit together!

Left: Billy and Marie pictured in 1975 at the staff dance.

Above: Billy's Kitchen Training Agreement and Certificate of Service.

Corridors of Fun

Living in was part of hotel life in the past and it was no different in the Central Hotel where managers had to live in the hotel as they were the resident licence holders. This meant that their children were brought up in the hotel environment. Can you imagine when being asked at school where you stayed and replying 'The Central Hotel.'

Above: John Nelson, third from the left in the front row, at a Hotel Managers' Meeting in 1962. All are dressed in dark suits and there's not one woman in their midst! Managers at the Central wore stripes until 6 pm and then had to be in dinner suits for the rest of the night.

Opposite, inset: The Beatles were among the celebrity guests at the hotel who were an everyday sight for the young Brendan and Iain.

That is the answer Brendan Nelson and his late brother, Iain, gave as the Central Hotel was their home for twelve years when their father, John, was the manager. Here are some of Brendan's memories:

" We lived in the Central from when I was six years old until I was seventeen (1955–1967). We came from Rothesay on the Isle of Bute where my brother Iain, who was eighteen months older than me, and I were born. Dad was then the manager of the Glenburn Hotel in Rothesay which was owned by Lord Bute.

Moving to Glasgow was a great adventure although at that age my brother and I had no idea what to expect. At the Glenburn we lived in a proper house in the hotel grounds and had lived a 'normal' life. Dad was Lieutenant Colonel John Watson Nelson MBE (Mil) and when he retired from the army he joined the Glenburn.

Dad was born in Thurso and we would regularly go there on holiday as children, visiting, of course, hotels owned by British Transport Hotels on the way, which had to include Gleneagles. He joined British Transport Hotels (BTH) in 1955. He was, as you would expect, very military in appearance and somewhat authoritarian. However, he was a real hotelier and under his management the Central became *the* hotel in the west of Scotland and the centre of most of the grand social activity in Glasgow. It was also *the* place to stay for visiting royalty, politicians, film stars, pop stars and the like.

Dad was always immaculately dressed and was very visible to all who stayed there. As I recall he became a bit of a personality in his own right. His boss was Étienne Vacher. My recollection was that Dad greatly admired him and they got on well together.

Life at the Central was pretty unusual for two young boys. We had a normal schooling and went to St Aloysius College, first to the preparatory school in Langside, so the hotel was handy for the train, and then to the secondary school at Garnethill which was within walking distance.

Living in a hotel had its advantages and disadvantages. The disadvantages were that there was nowhere to play and you had no neighbours. For playing we'd get a bus to Queen's Park but before we were old enough to do this we did kick a ball around and ride our bikes up and down the corridors (and tried to make sure Dad didn't catch us doing it). Mum joined in this little conspiracy!

The advantages were that we lived in comparative luxury with all the services of the hotel available to us. However this did not mean that my brother and I just picked up the phone every time we wanted something to eat. Mum tried to make our lives as normal as possible so she was in charge of food until our teenage years when, yes, we did order our own food on occasion.

We lived in a flat on the fourth floor right at the end of the Hope Street corridor. It had three bedrooms, a bathroom, kitchen, dining room and lounge. Mum used to cook whenever she could but provisions came from the hotel. There were certain traditions at that time, one of which was afternoon tea. When we arrived home from school every day a trolley would appear, piled high with sandwiches, scones and cakes and occasionally we would bring school friends back to share in this feast.

We were lucky to be at the hotel during the 'Swinging Sixties' when it was regularly used by all the visiting pop stars of the time. Most of them performed at the Odeon in Renfield Street which now stands empty. Every time a *big* group stayed, the front of the hotel was surrounded by fans so you could imagine how important Iain and I felt when we could pass through the police cordon, although sometimes it was hard to convince them that we actually lived there!

Stars we met were the Beatles (we got all their autographs), the Rolling Stones (I met Mick Jagger and Keith Richards in Mick's room and got their autographs), Brian Poole and the Tremeloes, Gerry and the Pacemakers, Cilla Black, Dusty Springfield and Bobby Vee. There were many more but they didn't have quite the attraction at the time of the Beatles or the Rolling Stones. Because we lived in the hotel, we would just find out which floor their rooms were on, then go and ask the floor waiter if they were there and then knock on the door!

When I left school, but before I started training as an accountant, I used to work in the hotel, firstly as a wages clerk and then in the control office. My job in the control office was to sit in a little booth either in the hotel dining room or in the Malmaison and prepare the bills for the customers.

We left the Central in 1967 and Dad had a brief stay at the Station Hotel in Perth before going to the Great Western Royal Hotel in Paddington. After that he left BTH and joined another hotel group and became the manager of the Pitlochry Hydro until his retirement to Glasgow. However his heart never left the Central and he would have been unbelievably saddened to see the hotel decline over the years as it did.

Iain also pursued a career in hotel management, and worked for a spell in the Central, and then catering but he died just over ten years ago.

I have been back to stay since the hotel was refurbished and it was really strange revisiting it after so many years. So much of it was familiar yet different. Champagne Central did not exist in my day. My Dad's office was down that corridor, the last room on the left before you got to the bar. The American Bar has gone and the stairs down to what was the Malmaison now go down to the hotel restaurant. My room for the night I stayed was on the third floor right at the end of the Hope Street corridor and just underneath our old flat on the fourth floor. "

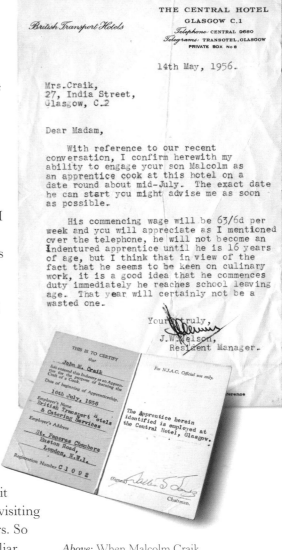

Above: When Malcolm Craik successfully applied to the Central for a position as an apprentice cook in May, 1956 it was to his mother John Nelson wrote confirming his appointment, as the would-be chef was only fifteen at the time. Malcolm's commencing salary was 63s 6d a week and he could not become an indentured apprentice until he reached the age of sixteen. The blue card, issued by the National Joint Apprenticeship Council of the Hotel and Catering Industry shows the official start of Malcolm 'learning the Craft of a Cook' in July 1956.

The BTH Reunion Club

Above: The BTH 1992 Reunion celebrated with a large iced cake.

Below: A letter of appreciation from a party of stranded air travellers who were brought back to Central Hotel and looked after when their flight to the USA was cancelled due to inclement weather, in December 1972.

A large hotel like the Central Hotel could be likened to a town in miniature. Like a town it never sleeps and its many departments are like the different areas of a town, each with their own politics, protocols and intrigues. The scriptwriters of *Eastenders* or *Coronation Street* would have been hard pushed to match the dramas taking place in the days when most of the Central Hotel staff lived in the rooms set aside for them in the top three floors of the building!

Many of the memories in this book have come from the 1970s, covering the last decade or so before the hotel passed from the hands of British Transport Hotels (BTH) into private ownership. Past staff are full of nostalgia when they reminisce about the way things were during their time in the Central. Some of the memories that many share include:

🍂 the pride they felt when job advertisements in the hotel industry carried the words 'Must be British Transport Hotels trained'

🍂 the opportunity they had, as part of a hotel group, to apply for work in BTH hotels elsewhere and how they always met up with someone they knew in the BTH family

🍂 the enjoyment of a good social life when the formality of work was left behind and they went off duty

🍂 Christmas parties for the children of staff, annual staff dances, bus trips, summer outings

🍂 the forging of many friendships which the passing of the years and distance have not diminished.

The hotel had its own social club, chaired by Head Barman Jack Dyce. One of the longest-serving associations with the Central belongs to this former barman. Jack began his Central Hotel career in 1933 by chipping lumps out of blocks of ice to cool the long drinks of guests and customers. Four years after his Second World War naval service and eighteen months spent in Australia, Jack returned to the Central, where he met Hotel Cashier Netta Baillie. The couple married in 1949 and when Netta left to have their son and daughter Jack continued at the Central until 1983, only to be made redundant two years after the hotel had been privatised. During their time with the Central, Jack and Netta crossed paths with Edward G Robinson, Mae West, Frank Sinatra, Judy Garland, Cary Grant and the Beach Boys to name but a few. Many years on, Jack and Netta became guests of honour at Grand Central's relaunch party. While this book was being researched and written, Jack became ill and sadly passed away in early December 2011.

In the spring of 1973, five members of the front office staff were all twenty-one within a few weeks of one another. Over the years Kate Pierce (nee Powell), Lynne Wilson (nee Nicolson), Nancy Brown (nee Scott), Flora Buthlay (nee Montgomery) and Leslie Craig all went their separate ways but stayed in touch. For their fortieth birthdays, in 1992, they decided to get together again in the Central and to find as many BTH staff as they could to come along and join them.

They formed the British Transport Hotel Reunion Club and around 150 people attended the first event with ninety per cent of them having worked at the Central. Since then they have reunited to mark their fiftieth and fifty-fifth birthdays and in March 2012 it will be their sixtieth and, happily, they will be returning to the Grand Central to see the hotel in all its former glory.

Organiser, Kate Pierce, originally from Liverpool, started at the hotel as a bookkeeper in September 1971 and became Head Cashier before she moved on to the Charing Cross Hotel in London in August 1977. The cashier's office in her day was just inside the front door, behind reception, with a window looking out onto Gordon Street. It was the perfect spot for seeing celebrities come in or crowds gathering outside to see them arriving. The autographs of Cliff Richard, Jimmy Savile, David Wilkie and Sacha Distel are some of the ones collected during her six years' employment in Glasgow.

One of her most memorable autographs came from Gilbert O' Sullivan. Kate was off duty and in the Community Room on the sixth floor with some other members of staff when the phone rang from Reception. Gilbert wanted his trousers pressed before his performance in Glasgow, was anyone prepared to do it? Kate and a housekeeper took on the responsibility of ironing the star's silk trousers and delivering them to his room. They were told by his manager to wait and thought a healthy tip was coming their way, but it was an autographed picture instead!

As well as the BTH Reunion Club there is also the more elite BTH Managers' Club which meets on a more regular basis.

Above: Jack Dyce pictured tending bar in Central Hotel during the 1960s.

Left: Jack and Netta at Gleneagles as they celebrate his ninetieth birthday in style.

Left: George Dyce – father of Jack Dyce – as Father Christmas, Central Hotel Christmas Party 1954. Pictured with 'Santa' are Jack and Eleanor – Jack(senior)'s children. George worked in the hotel as a lounge waiter and finally as Hotel Timekeeper. George is pictured (above) outside the Timekeeper's Office on Hope Street.

Underground, Overground

Below: Careful collection of glass, paper, plastic and cardboard in the hotel's subterranean recycling area.

Bottom: Maintenance Manager, Stevie Masterson.

A smooth supply of deliveries is essential to any business and that includes those in Glasgow's busy city centre. Access is sometimes extremely difficult in this area and even more so for the Grand Central Hotel since it is surrounded by four of the city's busiest thoroughfares, Hope Street, Gordon Street, Union Street and Argyle Street.

However, the hotel has an ace up its sleeve – well, underneath its substantial stonework to be more accurate. Just a few yards past Central Station's Union Street entrance is a passageway often ignored by the many people who have walked past it hundreds if not thousands of times, and behind its black gates is the answer to the delivery man's dilemma. Within the archways deep beneath the concourse and platforms of Central Station lie what the staff refer to as the hotel's 'storage bunkers' – rabbit-warren-like lengths of tunnels that can be accessed directly from the hotel and are big enough to store all the essentials needed to keep the hotel adequately stocked. The tunnels belong to Network Rail and they are continually monitored by CCTV to ensure that the only people down there are those who have been given permission to be there.

Several days a week between the hours of 7.30 am and midday suppliers bring in everything from thousands of bars of soap to the mountains of food required to keep the hotel's guests well fed and happy. Whether it is the lorries delivering the 9,000 turkeys and the hundreds of gallons of celebratory champagne that the hotel will need over the festive season or simply the laundry pick-up van, all those making deliveries must have access clearance.

Rubbish, of course, is no small issue when it comes to the smooth operation of the Grand Central and six days a week the refuse contractor's dustbin lorries remove the hotel's refuse, with tonnage and recycling rates closely monitored.

This unique system of hidden tunnels, built into the original structure deep under Central Station, provide the Grand Central with another very useful advantage over many other hotels in the city – every celebrity or dignitary from pop stars to politicians, and including Scotland First Minister Alex Salmond, can be slipped in and out under cover and away from the prying cameras of the media.

The Maintenance Team

Members of the Grand Central Hotel's maintenance team repair everything from the trivial to troublesome, day or night. Whether it is changing a light bulb in the Champagne Bar or clearing a blocked drain, they know every nook and cranny of the hotel's Victorian structure. Simple day-to-day maintenance includes at least twenty bedrooms receiving a daily check from top to bottom and just twelve months after opening many have already received a fresh lick of paint.

Looking after the drains that criss-cross their way into the main sewage system in Hope Street is a more demanding job. At 130 years old they are hardly designed with twenty-first-century waste in mind and modern detergents, thousands of gallons of water and some more unusual items find their way down into the murky depths of the system, including a lipstick which shot out like a bullet when a drain was unblocked!

All of this is part of a day in the life of Maintenance Manager, Stevie Masterson, whose railway hotel background stands him in good

Planning Permission

stead at the Grand Central. Part of the hotel's refurbishment included £6,000 spent on video equipment that scoured every basement drain to give a clear picture of what to expect once the hotel was up and running and although it was not a pretty picture, its revelations showed the money to be well spent. Decades of scaling on the inside of the cast-iron pipes had reduced their inner circumference by up to fifty per cent and the only way to deal with the problem is an annual water jetting and constantly keeping tabs on what is passing through the drainage system.

Because of the hotel's status as a Grade-A listed building, it has been a challenge to marry up modern technology and innovation with the need to adhere to current listed buildings' legislation. Some of the problems that have had to be addressed were updating the heating system when much of the pipe work and most of the radiators had to be retained and, following in the tradition of the hotel's historic links with John Logie Baird's pioneering TV pictures, ensuring the latest wi-fi communications can get through three-foot thick walls.

Back in 1883 hairdriers, laptops and mobile phone chargers were unheard of but electrically things have also moved on. Demands for more energy have had to be met but within the first twelve months of operation Principal Hayley have been looking at ways of becoming more environmentally friendly and they will be installing, without the public noticing, a system to reduce power consumption throughout the building. Even though there is a £30,000 outlay, the £15,000 a year saving on bills will pay dividends after just two years.

And with Stevie and his small team on hand to ensure even the smallest task is taken care of – including changing around twenty light bulbs on a daily basis without the help of a dedicated light bulb man like the hotel had in days gone by – the future looks bright.

When hotel chain Principal Hayley began to bring the former Central Hotel into the twenty-first century, one thing they were meticulous about was ensuring proper planning applications were in place. As the old Central Hotel was a Historic Scotland Grade-A listed building the last thing they wanted was to fall foul of the authorities over its refurbishment – unlike its former owners, British Transport Hotels (BTH), who did just that back in 1975. Having decided to clean up the outside of the hotel around the front entrance, they had set about the task with vigour. However, no sooner did they stand back to admire their handiwork than the heavy hand of officialdom in the shape of Glasgow District Council came down upon them. Far from being pleased with BTH's efforts at stone-cleaning and repointing, the council informed them they had come up short on three counts.

Firstly, they had failed to obtain planning permission to clean the decades of smoke and grime from the stone. Secondly, they had omitted to ask the then Secretary of State for Scotland, William 'Willie' Ross, Baron Ross of Marnock MBE, for his approval of the work to be carried out on a listed building. And, last but not least, planning officials decreed that the pointing work was not up to standard for a listed building and it would have to be redone.

Fortunately a planning sub-committee agreed to overlook the errors, though it was reported in the *Daily Record* that a letter expressing extreme regret that the work had been carried out without consent was sent to BTH. In the end all was well when BTH apologised for their misdemeanours and a formal planning application was lodged – albeit it ten months late!

Above: Central Hotel's newly cleaned stonework around the entrance indicates just how much soot and dirt had built up over almost a century.

Below: Glasgow City Chambers (pictured in 1957).

From Humble Beginnings ...

Working at the Central Hotel has often been the starting block from which a career to the very top of the hospitality industry has sprung.

🐾 David Levin is one of the country's top hoteliers, heading the London-based Capital Group Ltd with two hotels – the five-star boutique Capital Hotel in Knightsbridge which he built in 1971 and the nearby Levin Hotel which welcomed its first guests ten years later.

David Levin

From a very early age it was David's dream to build, own and manage his own hotel in London and it was in the Central that his passion for the hotel industry was fuelled when he started work as a junior waiter in the Malmaison.

It was 1952, he was sixteen and having stayed in hotels while on family holidays, he had come to think of all hotel managers as film stars because they dressed in dark suits and were always perfectly groomed. He set his sights on becoming a hotel manager himself and with all the confidence of a teenager phoned up the Central and asked if he could have an appointment with the manager at the time, Étienne Vacher.

Mr Vacher was a larger-than-life character who brought a continental influence to the food and ambience of not only the Central but others in the British Trust Hotels (BTH) group before he retired in 1965 as Chief Hotels Manager. David got his appointment and, on being asked what he wanted to do within the hotel trade by Mr Vacher, he naturally replied, 'I would like to be a hotel manager.'

He started as a junior waiter in the Malmaison under the supervision of Luigi Balzaretti, although his parents were not happy at their son dropping out of Glasgow Academy for a job in the hotel trade. 'Your mother and I are desperately disappointed that you have not got a profession – you are going to turn into a dropout,' said his father. But David had no intention of any such thing.

Working in the Malmaison was extremely hard work even for a fit teenager and he was at the beck and call of the higher-ranked waiters who took great pleasure in giving him the tasks no one else wanted. This meant cleaning and endlessly running up and down the thirty-seven steps between the restaurant and the kitchen, where he recalls sawdust on the floor and coal-fired stoves (the hotel converted to gas in the 1950s).

The restaurant operated incredibly late hours, catering for many of the celebrities who wanted to eat when they came back to the hotel after a performance and it wasn't unusual for guests to still be in the restaurant at 2 am. The full complement of staff would also still be there as no one was allowed to leave until the last guest had gone. An exhausted David often had to walk the five miles home to Pollokshields as the trams had long stopped for the night by this time.

There were many high-profile diners in his time there including Danny Kaye and Hugh Fraser who later became Lord Fraser of Allander. David never spoke to any of them – in fact he wasn't allowed to serve a guest until Luigi thought he was up to the task and gave him guidance on how to hold the serving dishes and what to say. The first words he ever uttered to a diner were 'Madam, do you wish stuffing?'

His pay was £1 7s 6d a week and his mum took a £1 off him for his keep. When she died many years later, the family found amongst her belongings the very first £1-note David had given her. Long before this time though his parents' disappointment at his choice of career had turned to pride in what he had achieved.

After graduating from the Scottish Hotel School in 1954, David became a manager with BTH and worked in several establishments including the Lochalsh Hotel in Kyle of Lochalsh overlooking Skye. In 1965 he bought a seven-bedroomed hotel in Berkshire which needed a lot of work on both its ambience and its food. Baking their own bread, serving good food and great coffee in front of cosy log fires did a lot to attract new guests and the success of this venture allowed David to move on to the Capital Hotel in Knightsbridge.

🐾 The Malmaison, once favoured by so many of the city's top people and visiting celebrities for its fine French cuisine, was assigned to the Central Hotel's history when the restaurant closed down. The name, however, was not to disappear from Glasgow forever, for six years later top Scots hotelier, Ken McCulloch, resurrected it when he set up a new hotel chain and called it the Malmaison.

Ken had already made his mark on the hotel and restaurant business in Glasgow through venues such as the Rogano, Charlie Parker's, La Bonne Auberge and One Devonshire, the unique hotel in Glasgow's West End, all of which he had built up then sold on.

He had a fondness for the Malmaison having worked within its walls as a trainee after joining British Transport Hotels in 1964. Under Head Chef Jean-Maurice Cottet, the young Ken started off in the larder before putting on the tall chef's hat which, on top of his tall frame, made him rather an imposing character. During his time working in the Central kitchens he learned the practices of Escoffier and cooking is something he enjoys to this day.

As a trainee he had to learn other aspects of the hotel industry. There was not just one, but several staff dining rooms, and this was where staff honed their skills as waiters before being allowed loose on the paying guests. In an era where formality ruled and rank and file never mixed this even applied to the staff dining areas. The black staff dining room was only for the upper echelons of the staff, those who wore black suits and held senior positions. It was a nervous young man who learned his waiting skills at mealtimes in this room – before putting them into practice in a restaurant or dining room filled by diners dressed to the nines for lunch or dinner in what was then an opulent part of Glasgow. Within this small area could be found the top restaurants of the times, such as the 101, Guys and the Grosvenor, where the casual dress code of today was still a long way off.

The hours were long and sometimes Ken worked the breakfast, lunch and dinner shifts and still had to get himself home to Blanefield. Despite the commitment required he loved then, and still does, the industry in which he has chosen to make a career.

'I just want to do, what I do, well,' he says – a principle which is followed by today's management of the Grand Central.

Ken McCulloch

When planning the first of a new chain of hotels in Glasgow in the early 1990s, Ken came up with the idea of reviving the Malmaison name with its long history in the city. He had to persuade the company directors that it was the right name for their new hotel as the direct translation of Malmaison from the French into English ('sick or bad house') did not particularly appeal to them! Having won his case, he spent £100 on registration fees, and the Malmaison name returned to Glasgow.

Ken was sad when the chain which grew from the name was sold on at the end of the 1990s at a time when he was concentrating his business interests in Monaco, which, in turn, led to his involvement in the Dakota group of hotels.

French Connections

Above: The British Transport Hotels' logo.

Right: Étienne Vacher.

Below: A pamphlet of epicurean menus produced by the Scottish Society of Epicureans to mark their tenth anniversary in 1965.

One of the longest-ever staff associations with the Central Hotel belongs not to a Scot but to a Frenchman! After initially training in the hotel industry in his native France, Étienne Vacher joined the London, Midland and Scottish Railway hotel services in 1925 and worked at Gleneagles and Turnberry before arriving at the Central where he was Hotel Manager between 1934 and 1955. He then became Chief Hotels Manager of British Transport Hotels, a post he held for ten years before he left to become MD of a company who managed hotels in Portugal. He died in 1984 in the Algarve.

After the Second World War he was made an Officier de l'Ordre de la Légion d'Honneur for his services as a member of the French co-ordinating committee in the west of Scotland. The Malmaison flourished under his influence, and as secretary of the Friends of France group he was involved in bringing fashion supremo Christian Dior to present his collection in Glasgow and Gleneagles in 1955.

He was also Honorary President of the Scottish Society of Epicureans which was established in 1955 for an elite group of diners (membership was limited to forty). Their dinners were usually held either at the Scottish Hotel School or at the Central Hotel. The menus were supervised by Étienne Vacher and the Hotel School's directors. One of its aims was to give chefs and waiting staff the opportunity of preparing and serving complex dinners.

The dinner held in the Central on June 7, 1956 and attended by the Danish Ambassador, His Excellency V De Steensen-Leth, was prepared in Copenhagen, flown to Prestwick and served in Glasgow! To mark the tenth anniversary of the Society, menus served over the decade of its existence were printed in pamphlet form.

After The Flood

While the bulk of this book focuses on the history of what is now the Grand Central Hotel, it would be remiss not to look into the future and no one is better placed to do that than Scott Taylor, Chief Executive of Glasgow City Marketing Bureau. As General Manager of the Central Hotel when it was owned by Friendly Hotels in the mid-1990s, he is well versed on why its reopening is of vital importance to Glasgow. While under his stewardship the Central made more than £1 million per year, returning a twenty-five per cent net profit.

However, in December 1996 disaster struck. Glasgow had been experiencing freezing weather conditions with temperatures falling as low minus 20 degrees centigrade. On December 30, a thaw set in and, while the rising temperatures brought more than a welcome respite from the cold, the following

day saw water pouring down from two giant water tanks in the roof space of the hotel after they and a mains water pipe burst. From 7 pm on the last evening of the year until 2 am on the first day of 1997, hundreds of thousands of gallons of water rained from the seventh floor all the way down to the leisure club in the basement. The swimming pool flooded, the lights went out and more than 600 Grand Room wine glasses that should have been filled with champagne to toast in the New Year were full of filthy water.

Thanks to firefighters from Glasgow's Cowcaddens Fire Station the deluge was brought to a halt in the early hours of New Year's Day, but not before damage in excess of £1 million had been caused, closing the hotel until March. Scott had to make a difficult call to his head office. 'Wishing your chairman a happy New Year while telling him 200 of his 254 bedrooms are under water does tend to stick in your mind,' he recalls.

However, no one could be happier about the rejuvenation of the famous building. Scott says the hotel has played a central role in the lives of Glaswegians for more than 100 years and there was a collective sigh of relief when Principal Hayley's scale of commitment became known. He says the company has transformed the Grand Central into a hotel of great distinction that gives a stylish nod to a bygone era when it was held in such high esteem by the people of the city of Glasgow.

Above: Now disused, the water storage tanks in the loft of Grand Central Hotel remain in place – dry as a bone!

Left: Scott Taylor says. 'The Grand Central, the Grande Dame of the world's most famous hotels, has entered her Belle Époque – a truly beautiful and majestic hotel in an era of Glasgow's renaissance.'

Restoring the 'Dishevelled Duchess'

When the architects first looked at the former Central Hotel, after Principal Hayley had purchased it, a number of issues became apparent. Although the building was worth preserving, Donald Crerar of Edinburgh-based Crerar and Partners, had never seen a trading hotel in such a state. A string of previous owners had spent little on maintaining the hotel and latterly had been so strapped for cash that if a light bulb blew in a bedroom, the room was simply closed off. During the late 1970s and 80s the hotel had taken a downmarket route and large rooms were sub-divided into smaller units to attract more guests, further diminishing the once proud property.

However, just like General Manager, Laurie Nicol, Donald Crerar fell in love with the place and says

From small acorns …
An oak finial from the main staircase
at Grand Central Hotel.

Stripped bare during refurbishment,
the stairs and endless corridors await
their new raiment

Above: The bath, complete with original taps, which was discovered on the fifth floor during Principal Hayley's 2010 renovation may well have been one of those used by members of the public other than the hotel staff– albeit unbeknown to the former Central Hotel's owners.

During the 1940 and 50s, due to the slum conditions many Glaswegians lived in, homes with bathrooms were pretty non-existent unless you were pretty well-off. Around the time of his marriage to wife Jean in 1950, Bill Hicks, father of the author, recalled telling a workmate of his joy at being able to purchase what was known as a 'single-end' flat in the city's Springburn area. A single-end was basic room and kitchen accommodation without a bathroom, but Bill's buddy told him how he could scrub up for a special night out in the luxury of the Central Hotel. If he went to the concierge at the entrance of the hotel and slipped him a couple of coppers, he'd see his way to showing him to the fifth floor where he could indulge in a bath full of piping hot water.

that making the structure wind-proof and water-tight was job number one. Next came making a record of the hotel's existing condition coupled with historical research to determine any original features requiring special protection.

What had not been envisaged was the discovery of damage to the property in the form of unsympathetic alterations which could almost be considered as vandalism. In Champagne Central overlooking Central Station concourse, for example, the original plan was to install the bar in the middle of the room, but as workers lifted a beer-stained carpet and layers of linoleum the marvellous marble floor that we can now see was revealed and plans were hastily altered to expose it. It was the same story in the Grand Room of Glasgow where a false ceiling had been installed by previous owners. Looking at the room today with its stunning high ceiling complete with ornate plaster work, it is difficult to believe that someone actually had the audacity to think it chic to cover up such workmanship.

With just eighteen months to turn the hotel from a derelict building into an operating business, significant effort was required from everyone from the architects down to the person who polished the final piece of brass-work just hours before the first guests arrived. As well as the work in the Grand Room and Champagne Central, 186 bedrooms with modern-day facilities were created as was a new business centre with 21 rooms available for meetings

and conferences, new lifts were installed and the kitchens moved from the basement to the ground floor. Where the Malmaison and La Fourchette once stood now stand the Tempus Restaurant and Deli Central with its modern and relaxed ambience. The Tempus still has the balcony that was once a main feature of the Malmaison and hanging from the roof are the Murano-glass chandeliers which once hung from the Grand Room ceiling. A new entrance leading in from the station concourse was also included in the plans.

The thousands of guests who have come through the doors of the Grand Central since the refurbishment are reaping the benefits, not only of those endeavours but also of the risks Principal Hayley took by investing £20 million during one the worst economic downturns in modern times.

The Grand Central is a Historic Scotland Grade-A listed building and along with Central Station is included in Glasgow's top fifty buildings in an architectural map guide. The guide says, 'This is a much beloved and superbly restored temple of the industrial age.'

Above: The marble floor of Champagne Central is uncovered during refurbishment, and awaits cleaning to reveal its full glory.

Above: Exquisite ceramic tiling remains in place on the walls of a communal bathroom in the old staff quarters.

Above: Remains of beautiful, hand-painted wallpaper still cling to the walls of the hotel's deserted staff quarters.

Below: Architect Donald Crerar's west elevation of Grand Central Hotel.

Below: Even the back stairs, closed off to public eyes, feature fabulous artisanship in the elaborate ironwork.

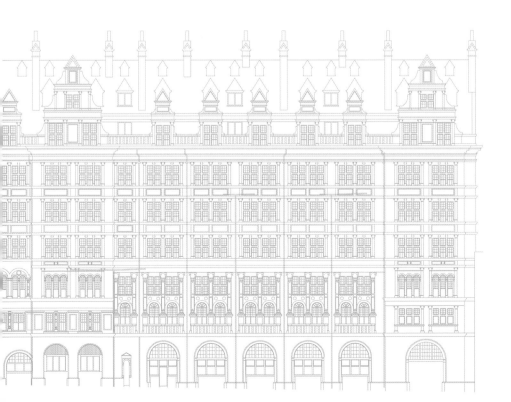

New for Old

Bringing the interior of the 130-year-old Central Hotel into the 21st century fell to Charles Leon and although first impressions last, thankfully the London-based designer saw past his initial thoughts which were, 'How did this hotel get into such a poor state of repair, especially since it had been in operation until a few months before Principal Hayley took over.' Peeling wallpaper, mould on the walls and bedrooms closed off by the dozen gave Charles the impression of a 'grand dame' having fallen into an almost irreversible nadir.

It seemed simply that after BTH sold the Central Hotel, it did not receive the investment necessary to keep the hotel up to date with the needs of the changing face of the hotel industry. Despite its good name for service, the surroundings were a little frayed, and with staff no longer living in, the hotel was not fulfilling its former glory.

However, Charles Leon Associates (C.L.A.) specialise in hotel interiors and, having worked on larger projects in terms of budget and scale, the challenge to bring the inside of the Central back to its former glory was one to relish. Although the budget was tight, the contractor responsible for the renovation was keen to turn the building back into a functioning hotel quickly and as a result the stripping out process began almost immediately. This allowed problems and condition to be speedily exposed, though it meant CLA had under four months to prepare their designs and drawings.

Top: Torn and faded wallpaper made way for new, designer decoration.

Right: The fully redecorated Grand Room of Glasgow as it appears today, and (above, right) as it was found pre-refurbishment with chandeliers, now hanging in Tempus Restaurant, and lowered ceiling.

Opposte page: The full extent of the damage to the crest above the fireplace was revealed during the refurbishment. The crest remains in place today, but hidden.

Dignity was a key word when it came to the finished plans. The intention was to return the 'Grand Dame' to her deserved status while ensuring her history remained intact. It was a particularly sad day when it was discovered the original Caledonian Railway Crest which once stood proud in the Grand Room of Glasgow had been badly damaged by fire in the 1970s. For now it remains on the wall but boxed over and out of sight. On the other hand, although the three chandeliers which once hung in what is now the Grand Room had sustained damage, by taking

parts from each of them, two were rescued and they now hang in the hotel's Tempus Restaurant.

The lamps that once lined the corridor leading to the Grand Room are now in the Ladies toilet on the Entresol level.

In line with Principal Hayley policy, most of the new furnishings, the wallpaper (the Grand Room of Glasgow got five-star treatment with a thistle-patterned wallpaper made specially for it) and even the chandelier in the main staircase were UK sourced and many of the colour schemes were inspired by Caledonian Railway themes.

It is impossible not to be impressed by the main chandelier which cascades down the central well of the main staircase. Manufactured by Northern Lights of Chesterfield, it is held up by giant steel beams installed above the ceiling.

Opposite page: A selection of shots displaying the hotel mid-refurbishment, as old furniture is stockpiled prior to disposal (left column). In the main pictures we see the 'Closing Party', held in the hotel before the majority of the refurbishment took place, as a farewell to the hotel in its late twentieth-century garb. Grey-wigged staff dressed in dusty tuxedos served drinks while a ghostly string quartet played; and a spectacular light show in the Grand Room of Glasgow showcased the old chandeliers.

Left: The ornate carving above the fireplace in the Grand Room of Glasgow.

Below: The Clyde Suite.

Before And After

Above: Champagne Central.

Below: An example of the bedrooms as a run-down room becomes part of a luxurious suite.

Before And After

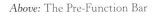

Above: The Pre-Function Bar

Below: Tempus Restaurant.

Grand Central Hotel Opening Team

Opening team including: James Anderson
Anna Dlugosz
Marie McGill
Natalie Simpson
Mark Duncan
Aneta Winnicka
Momina Asad
Emilia Wisniewska
Cherelle McGowan
Laurie Nicol
Tiernan Redmond
Lesley Reid
Clare Fairfield
Emma McCulloch
Claire Ferris
Leanne Scobie
Samantha Webster
Hilary Kerr
Fiona McPhail
Jill Wilson
Sue Howell
William McGowan
Wendy Johnston
Lynne Doyle
Douglas Campbell

Diane Ross
Georgina Docherty
Adam Cosgrove
Scott McLean, Saima Shafaatulla
Pauline Szabo
Nicola Thompson
Ross Mcleod
Chris Grant
Alex Rokhum
Chris Jenkins
Andy Hamilton
Barry Van den Berg
Chris Bruce
Sebastian Raneri
Yuri Afanasjev
Bethany Parker
Moray Nicol
Kevin Smart
Andrew McMillan
Wojciech Czech
Tommy Dunne
Claire Cuthbertson
Darren Campbell
Fabien Williamson
Stevie Masterson

What A Night It Was

On January 20, 2011 the Grand Central Hotel glittered, sparkled and almost burst with pride as it revealed itself in all its refurbished glory to the 1,200 guests attending the party to officially launch its comeback as one of the city's leading four-star hotels. Outside the temperature may have been hovering around minus but behind the walls of the Grand Central hearts warmed at the sight of the transformed hotel.

Among the guests were those who knew the hotel from times long gone by and some who had never crossed its threshold before but all were to be given a taste of the glamour and excitement of life behind the walls of 99 Gordon Street – both as it used to be in its heyday as the Central Hotel and, thanks to its refurbishment, as it was going to be for years to come as the Grand Central Hotel.

On arrival, guests were provided with a 'passport' indicating what was going on and where; and as they wandered from one entertainment to another many must have wondered what it would have felt like to have been around in the days when porters carried the luggage of celebrities such as Cary Grant, Mae West and Laurence Olivier for some of the biggest tips around. Although it must have seemed that some celebrities were actually there, alive and well in 2011, because impersonators of everyone from Charlie Chaplin to Laurel and Hardy and Humphrey Bogart were there to show everyone around.

As guests made their way into the Grand Room of Glasgow they were treated to canapés, oysters, sushi, the finest of wines and the best champagne Glasgow had to offer on that chilly January evening. There was music and dancing as the fizz

flowed but when everyone was in attendance in the Grand Room, the band stopped playing and the dancers stood still as all eyes turned to the stage.

Of the three people standing there, the first to speak was Grand Central Hotel's General Manager, Laurie Nicol. She painted a vivid picture of why she had fallen in love with the building the first time she walked through its doors, how she had set her heart on working to bring the place back to life and her hopes and dreams for the future of one of Scotland's most famous hotels. She was followed by the Principal Hayley Chairman, Roger Devlin. He spoke from the heart about why the company had chosen to invest so heavily in a piece of the Second City's heritage and his words met with unanimous approval and applause. Finally it was the turn of the third speaker to address the guests – none other than Scottish First Minister Alex Salmond. His presence spoke volumes about just how important retaining our national heritage is to the people of Scotland. First Minster Salmond addressed his task with wit, knowledge and passion, not only about what the reopening of the Grand Central Hotel meant to him personally, but also of its importance to the economies of Glasgow and Scotland.

Below: Ex-Miss Scotland Nieve Jennings.

Guests Enjoying the Launch Party

Among the guests looking on and listening were actor and platinum-selling singer-songwriter Darius, Glasgow's Lord and Lady Provost, representatives from Glasgow City Marketing Bureau, Glasgow Chamber of Commerce, clients and potential clients of the new hotel.

Once the speeches were over, the fun began as guests enjoyed a variety of activities as well as plenty of food and drink. For the whisky lovers there was whisky-tasting in the Clyde Suite with

Guests included: Katie Stewart, Elaine Taylor, Jane Irvine, Mirian Watson, Alex Campbell, Elspeth Campbell, Gayle Pike, Kim Baran, Tracey Atcheson, Tracey Reynolds, Lynn Lestner, Katy Thomson, Lyndsay Thomson, Donald MacLeod, Paul Lynch, Aileen Douthwaite, Douglas Campbell, Claire Lynch, Paul Donaldson, Doreen Douthwaite, Nieve Jennings.

Suite with samples of Talisker, Glenkinchie, Singleton and Dalwhinnie (courtesy of Diageo). For those suffering from the stress of Christmas, beauty and relaxation therapies were provided in the John Logie Baird, John F Kennedy and Robert Rowand Anderson Suites. Downstairs, Deli Central, once home to La Fourchette, provided top-notch food and modern music while in the Tempus Restaurant, formerly the Malmaison, there was a smooth jazz band with menu-tasters rekindling memories of the way things used to be. Back in the Grand Room, magicians and illusionists baffled with their sleight-of-hand tricks while trapeze artists took full advantage of the rediscovered ceiling height by providing a dazzling display of manoeuvres above the heads of their guests, all before an amazing vocal performance by Darius.

The party, which went on until the wee small hours, was enjoyed by all. It was an appropriately grand affair to mark the start of another era for the Grand Dame of Gordon Street. Everyone who attended was left with the knowledge that the future of the Grand Central Hotel was safe in the hands of Principal Hayley, the hotel team and everyone else who has been involved in creating this new and exciting chapter in the illustrious history of the Central Hotel.

Guests Enjoying the Launch Party

Guests included: Nigel Scullion, Jill Dinsmore, Donald MacLeod, Nicholas Scullion Snr, Lorraine Herbison, David Dinsmore, Darius Campbell, Darius' parents Avril and Booth, Helen Coles, Alex Salmond, Allan Nicol, Rodger Devlin, Lord and Lady Provost, Jack and Netta Dyce, Tiernan Redmond, Sandra Kerr, Lizzie Fisher, Denise Pinto, Lorna McGowan, Kat Lyons, Martin Stephen, Frances McMeeking.

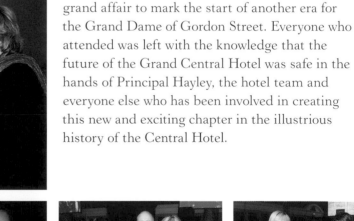

❧ Amongst those attending the Grand Central Hotel's glittering party on January 20, 2011, was was platinum-selling recording artist and actor, Darius Campbell, who has had more than a fleeting interest in the bygone days of the hotel.

His maternal grandparents have both passed away but the Central Hotel was a favourite place for

At the age of fourteen his grandfather worked in the shipyards of the war-time Clyde town, working hard and attending night school to became a mechanical engineer. He travelled the coast of Africa on a ship made in Greenock, while Darius' grandmother Rona became a nurse.

They loved nothing more than to visit the Central, says Darius, treasuring their times together there and the romantic sense of old Hollywood. As he took a tour of the hotel he wondered where they might have had tea, and

them in the 1940s and 50s where they enjoyed afternoon tea or had dinner to celebrate wedding anniversaries. It was to the Central they went to mark a very special occasion in their lives – the birth of Darius' mother, Avril, in 1952.

Memories of precious times spent in the splendour of the hotel in those days have been handed down to Darius through the generations. His grandparents – Colin and Rona Campbell – were both born in Greenock in 1924 and they married in February 1946. As a young couple they worked hard to build a home and it was not a life laced with the luxuries some newlyweds enjoy today.

which table they dined at while they enjoyed escaping from the hardships of the times and the world outside. The wonderful occasions spent there, says Darius, were happy times and little gems of luxury in their life together.

Since 2010 Darius has used Campbell as a surname in his professional career and, in 2012, it will be lit up in Broadway lights when he appears there as the youngest-ever Billy Flynn to perform in *Chicago*.

Above: Darius' grandparents Colin and Rona Campbell.

Left: Darius performing during the Relaunch Party at Grand Central Hotel.

And The Winner Is ...

The new-look four-star Grand Central Hotel and the hospitality it now offers have not gone unnoticed within the industry, with the hotel picking up a number of honours. In particular the Scottish Hotel Awards 2011 was an occasion for much celebration when the Grand Central was awarded the following:

Gold Laurel:	Principal Hayley Hotels for the Restoration of the Grand Central Hotel
Gold Medal:	Laurie Nicol (General Manager 2011)
Rising Star Event Venue of the Year:	The Grand Room of Glasgow
Friendly Service Award:	The Grand Central Hotel Team
Executive Chef of the Year:	James Murphy
Taste Award 2011:	Tempus Restaurant
Urban Bar of the Year:	Champagne Central
Glasgow Hotel of the Year:	The Grand Central Hotel
Rising Star Wedding Co-ordinator of the Year:	William McGowan
Banqueting Manager of the Year 2011:	Mark Duncan

In addition there have been well-deserved honours in a number of other awards, including a TripAdvisor Certificate of Excellence. TripAdvisor award this certificate to hotels which consistently receive excellent ratings from their members. The Grand Central was also a finalist in the Scottish Licensed Trade News Awards as Hotel of the Year for Scotland and it has a four-star accreditation from Visit Scotland and the AA. Principal Hayley in Scotland won Best Medium Group Hotel Employer as awarded by Caterer.com in their Best Employers in Hospitality Awards.

Opposite page, clockwise, from bottom left: Award winners with their gongs: James Murphy, Claire Cuthbertson and Adam Cosgrove, Zoltan Szabo, James Anderson and Mark Duncan.

Inset: Laurie Nicol with Adam Cosgrove

Main picture: The team – Mark Duncan, Banqueting Manager, James Anderson, Champagne Central & Banqueting bars Manager, Lesley Reid, Revenue Manager, Douglas Campbell, Regional Sales Manager, Barry Van Den Berg, Assistant Banqueting Manager, Laurie Nicol, General Manager, Scott McLean, Tempus & Deli Manager, Stevie Masterson, Maintenance Manager, Claire Cuthbertson, HR Manager, James Murphy, Executive Head Chef, Adam Cosgrove, Operations Manager, Clare Fairfield, Sales Manager Zoltan Szabo, Senior Sous Chef, Will McGowan, Wedding Coordinator, Wendy Johnston, Conference & Events Sales Manager, Hilary Kerr, Sales Manager.

This page, left, top to bottom: Award winners Laurie Nicol, Will McGowan, Mark Duncan and Wendy Johnston.

Below, and right: Grand Central Hotel proudly displays its collection of awards.

Reflections on Grand Central Hotel

As a Glaswegian who remembers when visiting stars lent their glamour to the hotel (and vice versa), I am delighted that the refurbished Grand Central Hotel is again hitting the high notes. I know that the Grand Central has rapidly established itself once more in the first rank of our hotels, and is again a by-word for sophisticated and warm Glasgow hospitality.

Bob Winter
Lord Provost of Glasgow

The Central Hotel has always been an integral part of city centre life and it's wonderful to see the relaunched Grand Central Hotel, one year on, reclaiming its position as one of our best loved, and most successful, hotels. Grand Central is a great addition to Glasgow's thriving hospitality business and is unique in both its history and location – I am sure it will continue to go from strength to strength and I wish Laurie and her team all the best for the future.

Stuart Patrick
Chief Executive,
Glasgow Chamber of Commerce

The Scottish Event Awards were extremely proud to have been the first event held in the newly refurbished Grand Central Hotel, on the 9th September 2010. The awards recognise and support the events industry in the country so for us it was an obvious place to host our awards, especially with the history and beauty associated with the hotel. It was a unique experience for myself and colleagues, to be able to work so closely with the Grand Central Management Team and share in the excitement. We saw the venue rapidly develop from a building site, where we had to don hard hat and wellies, right through to the elegance it has become today. As an event professional, this was the year I took a leap of faith that the venue would be ready in time for our awards and although the toilets were being fitted the night before and the bar prepared on the day, I never had any doubt that the Grand Central Team would deliver. We are delighted to have marked the re-opening of the Grand Central Hotel and confident that it has a prosperous future ahead, for many years to come.

Lynn Lester
Managing Director of Events,
Carnyx Group Limited

*After the rigours of travel
the bliss of journeys end
To surrender not merely one's
luggage, but one's self into the
keeping of others. To know that
your well being is as much
their concern as your own.
After the storm, calm seas …*

Hugh Leonard, Poet

From the moment I first stepped from the rattles and joggings of the sleeper train from London, wearily walked across the Station Platform into the completely embracing warmth and comfort of the newly refurbished Central Hotel it was obvious that Laurie Nicol and her team had put the 'Grand' back into the Grand Old Lady and true, gracious and welcoming hospitality had returned to where it belonged, in that wonderful building now correctly renamed The Grand Central Glasgow.

Grand Hotels are all about ladies and gentlemen serving and looking after ladies and gentlemen in a highly comfortable environment. The Grand Central now practises this in a seamless, efficient and strangely relaxingly vibrant style whether it is the sipping of champagne whilst watching the rigours and stress of the Station platforms below or munching the wonderful epicurean delights prepared by the Executive Head Chef James Murphy and his team in one of the many refurbished public rooms of the hotel or the comfort and privacy of your own hugely spacious and cosy bedroom. The Grand Central is just what the Grand City of Glasgow needs to welcome her guests from far and wide.

Stephen Carter OBE
Hotelier of the Year 2011

The Grand Central is a piece of Glasgow nostalgia wrapped up in a thoroughly up-to-date and stylish box. I took my parents to Champagne Central for a family celebration a couple of months after the reopening. The hotel had been the centre of the social lives of their youth but this was the first time they had been through the door in decades. The years rolled back as they slowly worked out what was where in the remodelled layout. Standing moist-eyed in the bar, my father said: 'This is where I saw your mother for the first time …'

David Dinsmore
General Manager,
News International

It is wonderful to see one of Glasgow's truly iconic buildings restored to its former glory. Since its refurbishment, the Grand Central Hotel has provided a luxurious setting for a number of fundraising events run by the Hospice and our guests are continually delighted by the beautiful surroundings and outstanding service.

Rhona Baillie
Chief Executive,
The Prince & Princess of Wales Hospice

The magnificent refurbishment of the Grand Central Hotel marks a welcome return for one of Glasgow's favourite landmarks. It's an iconic building full of fantastic memories and entertaining tales. What a stylish setting to build many new happy memories. And, for those of a sparkling disposition, where better to toast the renovation than the stunning Champagne Central.

Donald Martin
Editor,
The Sunday Post

Having such a vibrant and exciting hotel adjoining Glasgow Central Station is fantastic. Seeing the hotel being transformed on our doorstep under the new owners has been quite remarkable and they have done a truly amazing job. It now brings another dimension to the station and encourages new types of business and some interesting collaborations which will hopefully continue well into the future. The only downside is watching from my office as folk enjoy a drink in Champagne Central!

Nicholas Prag
Station Manager,
Glasgow Central

It's great to see a grand old building restored to such magnificent grandeur with a team who are committed to make it come alive for guests and visitors alike.

John Sharkey
Chief Executive Officer
SECC Ltd

I had the opportunity to work in the kitchen of Central Hotel over 40 years ago, the experience gained and the values that it instilled in me have stayed with me all my working career therefore to see the rebirth of the hotel as the 'Grand Central Hotel' after so many years is a marvellous achievement for which the Directors of Principal Hayley Hotels and the Management and Staff of the Grand Central are to be congratulated.

Neil Thomson
Chief Executive,
Federation of Chefs Scotland

We were delighted to be one of the first organisations to hold our Christmas event at the newly refurbished Grand Central Hotel back in 2010. There was a great deal of expectation knowing we were coming to a party at one of the oldest hotels in Glasgow. The conference rooms used to plan the party were modern and accommodating which helped the committee meetings run smoothly. On the night of the party, the first impressions were absolutely fantastic and the grand corridors decked out with Christmas decorations, coupled with the magnificent Champagne Central, all added up to a fantastic event. The HIT event at the Grand Central was excellent, so much so, we have just had another annual party there this year. The professionalism of the staff, coupled with a great meeting and event venue, add up to a truly unique hotel that will be part of the Glasgow scene for years to come.

David Cochrane
Chief Executive,
HIT Scotland

Glasgow's top newspapers salute this grand gesture to a great hotel.

Tim Blott
Managing Director,
Herald & Times

The Grand Central Hotel is a fantastic example of Scotland's commitment to providing a quality visitor experience.

Mike Cantlay
Chairman,
VisitScotland

The Grand Central Hotel, restored to surpass even its original glory, remains not just a jewel in the crown of Glasgow but provokes wonderful nostalgic memories for myself and my family. A Glaswegian born and bred, the Central was an integral part of growing up in the city. My parents were married in the Central Hotel, I attended my 10-year school reunion there and I have fond memories of its flagship restaurants the Malmaison and La Fourchette. I was thrilled to organise one of the first events in the newly refurbished Grand Room of Glasgow – a sell-out fashion show in aid of the Princess Royal Trust for Carers. I am proud to host many Institute of Directors events with business and political leaders in the Hotel and enjoy meeting friends and colleagues in the magnificent Champagne Central overlooking the station concourse.

Laura Gordon
Chairman,
Institute of Directors,
Glasgow and West of Scotland

Acknowledgements

The authors and publisher would like to say a special thanks to Jim MacIntosh of the Caledonian Railway Association, Kate Pierce of the British Transport Hotels Reunion Club, Bob Bain of the Scottish Music Hall Society, Brian Donald, freelance writer and boxing historian, staff at the Glasgow University Archives where the Caledonian Railway Association Archives are kept and the staff at the Mitchell Library, in particular Christine McGilly. To all of you, your patience, help and interest in the compiling of information and pictures for this book was just brilliant!

We would also like to sincerely thank Tim Blott, Managing Director of the Herald and Times Group, who gave permission for many of the staff pictures of celebrities taken at the hotel over many decades to be used in this book. This gesture is much appreciated.

We would like to thank the General Manager of the Grand Central, Laurie Nicol, and all her staff who extended a warm hand of hospitality to us for four months, patiently putting up with our presence and questions whilst trying to get on with their work, and allowing us the freedom to explore this magnificent building in order to get a glimpse of its life in the past and in the present. We say a glimpse because, as each day went speedily by, we realised we were uncovering a lot of information but there was much, much more which still could be told.

We are also very grateful to the many individuals who have contributed their stories and/or their personal mementoes of the Central Hotel to this book. They include:

Anna Bain, Malcolm Bain, Malcolm Baird, Beryl Beattie, Bob Burnett, James Cairns, Billy and Marie Campbell, Mark and Michael Carlin, Jessie Clark, Clive Coates, Leslie Craig, Malcolm Craik, Donald Crerar (Crerar & Partners Architects), Tom and Jacqueline Donnelly, Linda Falls, Angus Farquhar, Peter Fort, Patricia Fraser, Jimmy Friel, Walter Frintrop, Marilyn Gaya, Reverend Tom Gillies, Norrie Gilliland, Iain Gordon, Ian G Grant, Nan Grimstead, Elizabeth Lauder Hamilton, Gordon Henderson, Iain Henderson, Ian Holland, Jeff Horner, Stephen Johnson, Elizabeth Joyce, Vicki and Robin Lee, Charles Leon, David Levin, Tom Love, Desmond Lynn, Ken McCulloch, Bob McDonald, Charlotte McEleney, Alastair McFarlane, Jim MacIntosh, Gordon McKenzie, Sharon and Allan Mackin, Eileen McManus, Jean McMillan, Wilma Matthew, Bill Matthews, Ritchie Miller, Alex Morrison, Andrew and Ann Muir, Richard Muir, Candy Munro, Margaret Munro, Brendan Nelson, Allan Nicol, Brian Nugent, Joyce Parrack, Kate Pierce, Nicholas Prag, Brian Presswell, Joyce Reid, John Scott, Isa Scougall, Jim Slavin, Una Smith, Cynthia Spillman, Steiner Family, Anne and Leslie Stewart, Scott Taylor, Chris Thornhill, Nelson Twells, Terry Martin's special friend Valerie M Walker, Stuart Wallace, Denis Woodtli. Special thanks to recording artist and actor, Darius, for contributing his memories of his grandparents, Colin and Rona Campbell, who loved to celebrate their wedding anniversaries in the Central Hotel.

We are grateful to the following individuals and organisations for their contributions to the artwork of this book:

Euan Adamson: p93, bottom left and right

Automobile Club de Monaco: p81, bottom right

Andy Barr: p158, top right

Bygum Records: p133, left

Caledonian Railway Association: p22; p24, bottom right; p25 (all); p26 (all); p27, top left; p29, bottom right; p32 (all); p35, bottom left; p36; p54 (all); p55, top and centre; p73, four on right; p74 (all); p76, left

Clyde 1: p120, top and bottom right, bottom left

The Daily Record: p105, bottom right; p111, top right; p118, bottom left

Jack and Eleanor Dyce: p133, all except bottom left

Stephen Fisk: p30, bottom left

fmua: p72, bottom right, courtesy of shutterstock.com

Rev Tom Gillies: p41, bottom centre

Glasgow City Libraries, licensor scran.ac.uk: p30, top

The Gospel Truth Choir: p121, top right, artwork by Bill Matthews/Michael Murray

Grand Central Hotel: pp10/11; p39, right; p41, top left; p 43, top left and right; p57, top right; p123, right; p125, bottom right; p126 (all); p127, top right, bottom left and right; p130; p143, top left; p144, top right, bottom left; p146 left bottom three; p148, top right; p149, top left, bottom right; p152, top left

Richard Griffin: p46, top left

The Herald and Evening Times Archive: p34, bottom right; p43, bottom; p45, top left; p51, top left; p57, left; p58(all); p59, top and bottom left; p84; p85; p87, right; pp88/9; p90 (all); p91; p94, top left; p95; p96 (all); p97; p99 (all); p101 (all); p102; p103, top and bottom left; p104, bottom; p135

The Herald and Times Group: p56/7; p64

Thurston Hopkins/Stringer: p121, top left, courtesy of Getty Images

Lagui: p71, left, courtesy of shutterstock.com

Ledzeppelin.com: p106, top left

Milos Luzanin: p112, top left, courtesy of shutterstock.com

The Harry Margolis Entertainment Organistaion: p160, bottom left inset

Dean McKeown, Sons of the Desert: p93, top and far left

Adrian B McMurchie: p59, top right

Mark Mechan: p11, right; p16, top centre; p20, bottom; p21, top left; p23, right; p33, top; pp38/9; p50, top left; p63, bottom; p75, bottom left; p92, bottom left; p124 (all); p134 (all); p139 all; pp140/1; p142, top left; p143, top and bottom right; p144, top left; p145, top left; p156 top right

Mitchell Library Special Collections: p117, right

Morrison Boxing Promotions: p114, bottom right

National Library of Scotland: p31

nisbetwylie.com: p137

NVA: p68 (all); p69 (all)

pseudolongino: p54, top, courtesy of shutterstock.com

RCAHMS (Henry Bedford Lemere Collection), licensor rcahms.gov.uk: p27, bottom right; p28; p35, top and bottom right

Science and Society Picture Library: p116 (all); p117, left

Jill Scott: p8; p54; p65, bottom

Scottish Daily Express: pp52/3; p100, top

Lloyd Smith: p121, bottom right

Solo Syndication: pp82/3

Studio Canal: p120, top left

Sunshinephotography.co.uk: p.12 (all); p13; p14, middle and bottom centre; pp14/5; p16, top left and bottom; pp16/7; p18/9; p20, bottom; p21, top and bottom right, bottom left; p29, top right; p37; p127, top left; p144, bottom right; p146, top; p148, top left and bottom right; p149, top right and bottom left

Ming Tang-Evans: p136

D C Thomson & Co Ltd, Dundee: p34, bottom left; p46, bottom left; p47(all); p49, bottom left; p62 (all); p75, top right; p77, top and middle right; p86, top left and centre; p92, bottom right; p98, top left, top and bottom right; p105, top left; p107, middle right; p111, bottom left, centre, bottom right; p112, bottom left; p114, top right; p119, top right; p131, centre

Topal: p9, courtesy of shutterstock.com

UEFA: p78, right

University of Glasgow Archive Services, House of

Fraser Collection: p60 (all); p61 (all)

V&A Publishing: p121, bottom left

Lenny Warren/Warren Media: p6; p7; pp150/51; p152, top right, bottom left and right; p153 (all); p154 (all); p155, left and centre; p156 (all); p157 (all)

Wellcome Library, London: p115, bottom left

Chris Watt: p159, top right

Simon Williams Photography: p147 (all)

Neil Wilson: p115, top right

Graham Wylie: p137

Bibliography

Dior by Dior, The Autobiography of Christian Dior. V&A Publications 2007.

Glasgow's Forgotten Village: The Grahamston Story. Norrie Gilliland. Grahamston Publications 2002.

The Scots-Italians. Joe Pieri. Mercat Press 2005.

Centenary of the Caledonian Railway 1847–1947. Published by the London, Midland and Scottish Railway. September 1947.

The Caledonian Edinburgh. Andreas Augustin and Roddy Martine. The Most Famous Hotels in the World.

The Glasgow Encyclopedia. Joe Fisher. Mainstream Publishing 1994.

The Second City. C A Oakley. Blackie and Son, Ltd. 1967.

Dating Old Photographs. Robert Pols. Federation of Family History Societies 1995.

Scottish Architects' Papers, A source book. Rebecca M Bailey. The Rutland Press 1996.

Collins Encyclopaedia of Scotland. John Keay and Julia Keay. Harper Collins 1994.

Glasgow. David Daiches. Andre Deutsch 1977.

Portrait of Glasgow. Maurice Lindsay. Robert Hale and Company 1972.

Glasgow 1881–1885. Vital, Social and Economic Statistics of the City. James Nicol. The Grimsay Press 2003.

Twentieth-Century Scotland, A Pictorial Chronicle 1900–2000. Edited by Martin Hannan and Donald MacLeod. Mainstream Publishing 2000.

Lost Glasgow: Glasgow's Lost Architectural Heritage. Carol Foreman. Birlinn 2002.